Personal Best

A2 Elementary

Student's Book and Workbook combined edition **A**

Series Editor
Jim Scrivener

Student's Book Author
Louis Rogers

Workbook Author
Genevieve White

STUDENT'S BOOK CONTENTS

		LANGUAGE			SKILLS	
		GRAMMAR	PRONUNCIATION	VOCABULARY		
1 You and me 1A Meeting and greeting p4 1B My summer blog p6 1C Is that a man bag? p8 1D Where's my wallet? p10		• the verb *be* • possessive adjectives • *'s* for possession	• contractions of *be* • sentence stress	• countries and nationalities • numbers 1 – 1,000 • personal objects	**READING** • a blog about a summer spent in London • approaching a text • simple statements with *be*	**SPEAKING** • asking for and giving personal information • asking for clarification **PERSONAL BEST** • a conversation in a lost property office
2 Work and play 2A What I do p12 2B Weekdays, weekends p14 2C Find a flatmate p16 2D A new city p18		• present simple: positive and negative • present simple: questions	• *-s* and *-es* endings • auxiliary verbs *do/does* in questions	• jobs and job verbs • activities (1)	**LISTENING** • a video looking at work and free-time activities • listening for names, places, days and times • introduction to the sound /ə/	**WRITING** • opening and closing an informal email • connectors: *and, but* and *or* **PERSONAL BEST** • an email to a friend

1 and 2 — REVIEW and PRACTICE p20

3 People in my life 3A Time together p22 3B A new group p24 3C Opposites attract p26 3D A night out p28		• adverbs and expressions of frequency • *love, like, hate, enjoy, don't mind* + noun/*-ing* form	• sentence stress • *-ing* forms	• family • activities (2)	**READING** • a website about local clubs and groups you can join • scanning a text • *also* and *too*	**SPEAKING** • making arrangements • accepting or declining an invitation **PERSONAL BEST** • making arrangements with a friend to do an activity
4 Home and away 4A 24 hours in the dark p30 4B Weather around the world p32 4C A long weekend p34 4D A holiday with friends p36		• prepositions of time • present continuous	• sentence stress • linking consonants and vowels	• daily routine verbs • the weather and the seasons	**LISTENING** • a video about the weather in different parts of the world • listening for the main idea • sentence stress	**WRITING** • describing a photo • using personal pronouns **PERSONAL BEST** • an email describing a holiday

3 and 4 — REVIEW and PRACTICE p38

5 What are you wearing? 5A Party time p40 5B Don't tell me what to wear p42 5C Do the things you love p44 5D Can I try it on? p46		• present simple and present continuous • *can* and *can't*	• dates • *can* and *can't*	• clothes • ordinal numbers • hobbies	**READING** • an article about uniforms and if we like wearing them • identifying facts and opinions • adjectives	**SPEAKING** • shopping for clothes • offering help **PERSONAL BEST** • a conversation in a clothes shop
6 Homes and cities 6A A small space p48 6B Amazing homes p50 6C The Big Apple p52 6D Beautiful places p54		• *there is/there are, some/any* • prepositions of place • modifiers	• *there's/there are* • sentence stress	• rooms and furniture • common adjectives • places in a city	**LISTENING** • a video about unusual homes • identifying key points • contractions	**WRITING** • topic sentences • describing places **PERSONAL BEST** • a description of your town or city

5 and 6 — REVIEW and PRACTICE p56

Grammar practice p112   Vocabulary practice p136   Communication practice p158   Irregular verbs p176

Language App, unit-by-unit grammar and vocabulary games

WORKBOOK CONTENTS

		LANGUAGE		SKILLS	
	GRAMMAR	PRONUNCIATION	VOCABULARY		
1 You and me 1A p2 1B p3 1C p4 1D p5	• the verb *be* • possessive adjectives and *'s* for possession	• contractions of *be* • sentence stress	• countries and nationalities and numbers 1–1,000 • personal objects	READING • approaching a text	SPEAKING • asking for and giving personal information
1 REVIEW and PRACTICE p6					
2 Work and play 2A p8 2B p9 2C p10 2D p11	• present simple: positive and negative • present simple: questions	• *-s* and *-es* endings • auxiliary *do/does* in questions	• jobs and job verbs • activities (1)	LISTENING • listening for names, places, days and times	WRITING • opening and closing an informal email
2 REVIEW and PRACTICE p12					
3 People in my life 3A p14 3B p15 3C p16 3D p17	• adverbs and expressions of frequency • *love, like, hate, enjoy, don't mind* + noun/*-ing* form	• sentence stress • *-ing* forms	• family • activities (2)	READING • scanning a text	SPEAKING • accepting or declining an invitation
3 REVIEW and PRACTICE p18					
4 Home and away 4A p20 4B p21 4C p22 4D p23	• prepositions of time • present continuous	• sentence stress • linking consonants and vowels	• daily routine verbs • the weather and the seasons	LISTENING • listening for the main idea	WRITING • describing a photo
4 REVIEW and PRACTICE p24					
5 What are you wearing? 5A p26 5B p27 5C p28 5D p29	• present simple and present continuous • *can* and *can't*	• dates • *can* and *can't*	• clothes and ordinal numbers • hobbies	READING • identifying facts and opinions	SPEAKING • offering help
5 REVIEW and PRACTICE p30					
6 Homes and cities 6A p32 6B p33 6C p34 6D p35	• *there is/there are, some/any* and prepositions of place • modifiers	• *there's/there are* • sentence stress	• rooms and furniture • common adjectives • places in a city	LISTENING • identifying key points	WRITING • topic sentences
6 REVIEW and PRACTICE p36					

Writing practice p74

UNIT 1

You and me

LANGUAGE   the verb *be* ■ countries and nationalities ■ numbers 1–1,000

1A Meeting and greeting

1 What country are you from? Name three more countries near your country.

2 A Match the countries in the box with maps 1–6.

Italy   Germany   Turkey   the USA   Brazil   Japan

 1 _____
 2 _____
 3 _____
 4 _____
 5 _____
 6 _____

B ▶ 1.1 Listen. Write the letter of each speaker next to the correct map.

3 ▶ 1.1 Listen again. Write the nationality of each country in exercise 2.
the USA – American

Go to Vocabulary practice: countries and nationalities, page 136

4 A In pairs, look at the pictures. Where do you think the people are from?

B Read the conversations in exercise 5 and match them with pictures a–c.

a _____

b _____

c _____

5 ▶ 1.3 Listen and complete the conversations.

1		2		3	
Emilia	Hello. My name's Emilia and this is Sara.	**Sam**	Oscar, this is Meiko. ⁴_____ from Japan. And Meiko, this is Oscar. ⁵_____ from Brazil.	**Jo**	Hi, Ali. How are you?
Sabine	Hi, ¹_____ Sabine. Nice to meet you.			**Ali**	Very well, thanks. And you?
Emilia	You, too. Where ²_____ from?	**Oscar**	Nice to meet you, Meiko.	**Jo**	I'm fine. Where are Jean and Paola?
Sabine	I'm from Germany. And you?	**Meiko**	You, too, Oscar.	**Ali**	They aren't here. ⁷_____ in the conference centre.
Emilia	³_____ from Italy, from Milan.	**Oscar**	How do you spell your name?	**Jo**	What about Andreas?
Sara	I'm not! I'm from Rome.	**Meiko**	⁶_____ M-E-I-K-O.	**Ali**	⁸_____ here. His train's late.

4

the verb *be* ■ countries and nationalities ■ numbers 1–1,000   LANGUAGE   1A

6 Choose the correct forms of *be*. Use the conversations in exercise 5 to help you. Then read the Grammar box.

'm not   's   isn't   'm   're   aren't

1 I am = _____
2 you / we / they are = _____
3 he / she is = _____
4 I am not = _____
5 you / we / they are not = _____
6 he / she is not = _____

Grammar   the verb *be*

Positive:
I**'m** from Italy.   She**'s** Japanese.   We**'re** German.

Negative:
I**'m not** from Spain.   He **isn't** here.   They **aren't** American.

Questions and short answers:
Are you from Spain? Yes, I **am**. No, I**'m not**.   **Is** Andreas here? Yes, he **is**. No, he **isn't**.

Go to Grammar practice: the verb *be*, page 112

7 A ▶1.5 **Pronunciation:** contractions of *be* Listen and repeat the contractions.

I'm   you're   he's   she's   it's   we're   they're

B ▶1.6 Say the sentences. Listen, check and repeat.
1 I'm American and they're Brazilian.
2 He's Irish.
3 You're Swedish and we're Turkish.
4 She's from Russia.

8 Complete the sentences with the correct form of *be*. Use contractions if possible.
1 Pedro _____ Brazilian. He _____ from Recife.
2 My parents _____ from Poland.
3 Dublin _____ in the UK. It _____ in the Republic of Ireland.
4 '_____ your name Carlos?' 'No, it _____ Carlo.'
5 '_____ you from Mexico?' 'No, I _____. I _____ from Peru.'

9 In pairs, look at the pictures. What countries are the people from? What nationality are they?

A This is …   He's American.   **B** No, he isn't. He's Canadian!

a   b   c   d   e

Go to Communication practice: Student A page 158, Student B page 167

10 Write the words or numbers.
1 ____ twenty-five
2 36 _____
3 ____ a hundred and forty-three
4 364 _____
5 ____ seventy-seven
6 634 _____
7 ____ two hundred and eight
8 908 _____
9 ____ a thousand
10 894 _____

Go to Vocabulary practice: numbers 1–1,000, page 136

11 In pairs, introduce yourselves to each other. Say your age if you want to.

Hello. My name's …   You, too.   I'm …   I'm … years old.
Nice to meet you.   Where are you from?   How old are you?

Imagine that you meet a famous person. Write the conversation. Introduce yourself and ask him/her about himself/herself.

5

1 SKILLS READING approaching a text ■ simple statements with *be*

1B My summer blog

1 Do you like sport? What's your national sport? What sports do people usually do in the summer?

> **Skill   approaching a text**
>
> Before you read a text, predict as much information as you can.
> - Read the title of the text. Can you guess what it means?
> - Are there any pictures? What people, places and things can you see?
> - Are there any headings for the different sections? What are the sections about?

2 Read the Skill box. In pairs, look at the title, headings and pictures in the text. Answer the questions.
1 What type of text is it?
2 Who is the text about?
3 Where is she at the moment?
4 What is she doing there?

3 Read the text. Choose a title for each post.
1 Week 1   a Time to go home
2 Week 2   b Learning English
3 Week 3   c My British family
4 Week 4   d Enjoying the tournament

4 Read the text again and answer the questions.
1 What is María's nationality?
2 Where are Helen and Alex from?
3 What are María's favourite places in London?
4 Who is Hitoshi?
5 Where is María's English teacher from?
6 Where are the teams in the tournament from?
7 When are the matches?

5 Find words in the text to match the pictures.

1 h_____ f_____   2 c_____   3 t_____

4 m_____   5 c_____

> **Text builder   simple statements with *be***
>
> Simple statements with *be* have this pattern: subject + verb + complement:
> This is my blog.
> The teams are from Spain, Brazil, Portugal, Poland, Russia, England, Scotland and Japan.

6 Read the Text builder and look at the Week 1 post in the text again. Draw a box around the subjects, circle the forms of *be* and underline the complements.

7 In pairs, think of a sport you love. Tell your partner about it.
I love … It's really …

approaching a text ■ simple statements with *be*   READING   SKILLS   1B

María Gómez
My month in London

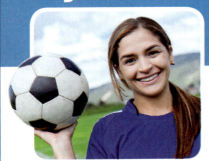

Hello! I'm María Gómez. I'm 21 years old and I'm from Cádiz in Spain. I'm a student and I love football! At the moment, I'm in the UK. I'm at a language school to learn English, but I'm also here for an international football tournament for students! This is my blog about my month in London.

Week 1

This is my host family. They're very nice. Helen's English and Alex is Scottish, and their children are called Jenny and Jacob. Jenny's fourteen and Jacob's twelve. Sometimes I play football in the park with Jenny and Jacob, and sometimes we all go for a walk in the centre of London. It's a really interesting city. My favourite places are Big Ben, Buckingham Palace and Tower Bridge.

Week 2

This is my language school. There are lots of students from different countries and we all speak English together. My classmates are really friendly. I always sit with Hitoshi. He's Japanese. Our English lessons are fun! Our teacher's name is Kerry and she's from Australia.

Week 3

I'm at the football tournament now. The teams are from Spain, Brazil, Portugal, Poland, Russia, England, Scotland and Japan. We train every morning. I think we're a good team because we're very fast. The matches are in the evening. They're really exciting!

Week 4

We're the champions! ☺ I'm happy, but I'm also sad because it's the end of my month here. Goodbye, London! Until next time!

Personal Best How many examples of the verb *be* can you find in the text?

1 LANGUAGE possessive adjectives ■ 's for possession ■ personal objects

1C Is that a man bag?

1 In pairs, look at the pictures in the text below. Can you name the objects?

2 A Read the text. Do you think the objects in the list are from a handbag, a 'man bag' or both?

B ▶ 1.8 Listen to a radio programme. Tick (✓) the objects that you hear.

His bag or her bag?

Where do you put your things when you go out? If you're a woman, your things are probably in your handbag, but what about men? Today, 50% of men also have a bag – a 'man bag'. Is a man bag the same as a handbag? And what do men and women carry in their bags?

	HANDBAG	MAN BAG
keys	☐	☐
chewing gum	☐	☐
hairbrush	☐	☐
gloves	☐	☐
sweets	☐	☐
tablet	☐	☐
umbrella	☐	☐
phone	☐	☐
wallet	☐	☐
purse	☐	☐

Go to Vocabulary practice: personal objects, page 137

3 ▶ 1.11 Listen to the start of the radio programme again and choose the correct options.

> **Presenter** Zoe's here with ¹ *she / her* handbag and Harry's here with ² *he / his* 'man bag'. What's in ³ *their / they* bags? Zoe, you first. What's in ⁴ *you / your* handbag?
> **Zoe** Let's have a look. Here are ⁵ *I / my* keys and ⁶ *my / me* hairbrush.

4 A Look at exercise 3 again. Then read the Grammar box. Which possessive adjective is for things that belong to:

1 a man? _____   2 a woman? _____   3 more than one person? _____

B Are possessive adjectives the same or different with singular and plural nouns?

📖 Grammar possessive adjectives

I	my	*my* bag/bags
you	your	*your* umbrella/umbrellas
he	his	*his* pen/pens
she	her	*her* glove/gloves
it	its	*its* photo/photos
we	our	*our* key/keys
they	their	*their* tablet/tablets

Go to Grammar practice: possessive adjectives, page 113

8

possessive adjectives ■ 's for possession ■ personal objects

LANGUAGE 1C

5 A ▶1.13 **Pronunciation:** sentence stress Listen and repeat the sentences. <u>Underline</u> the stressed words in each sentence.
1 What's in your handbag?
2 Here are my keys.
3 His sunglasses are on the table.
4 What's their phone number?

B ▶1.14 Practise saying the sentences. Listen, check and repeat.
1 Your tablet's new.
2 Where's my umbrella?
3 Here are our photos.
4 Her gloves are blue.

6 Complete the sentences with a subject pronoun or a possessive adjective.
1 My friends are Scottish. _____'re from Aberdeen.
2 **A** Where are _____ sunglasses?
   B On your head!
3 _____'m Spanish. Here's _____ identity card.
4 _____ name's Ahmed. He's 32 years old.
5 They're from Italy. _____ names are Francesca and Marco.
6 This is Harry. _____'s from London.
7 We're in the baggage area at the airport, but are _____ bags here?

7 Look at the sentences. Complete the rules about possession. Then read the Grammar box.
1 It's Carl's bag.
2 It's my sister's phone.
3 They're my friends' umbrellas.

After a singular name (e.g. *Mary*), we add ____.
After a singular noun (e.g. *girl*), we add ____.
After a regular plural noun (e.g. *boys*), we add ____.

Grammar 's for possession

For a singular noun or name:
Mary's glasses are in her bag.

For a plural noun:
My parents' car is red.

Irregular plural nouns:
The children's toys are everywhere!

Go to Grammar practice: 's for possession, page 113

8 ▶1.15 Look at the picture and listen to John and Mary. Match the possessions with the people in the box.

John   Mary   John's friends   Mary's sister   Carl

9 Choose the correct options to complete the sentences.
1 It's *Lucy's bag / Lucy bag*.
2 They're *Harry's / Harrys'* glasses.
3 I'm an English teacher. Here are all my *student's / students'* books.
4 It's my *friends' / friend's* phone. Look, this is his photo.
5 Here are the *mens' / men's* umbrellas.

Go to Communication practice:
Student A page 158, Student B page 167

10 A In groups of three to five, follow the instructions.
Student A: Close your eyes.
Other students: Put one of your possessions on the table.
Student A: Open your eyes. Guess whose things are on the table.

Is it Manuel's watch?   *Are they Maria's glasses?*

B Repeat the activity. Take it in turns to be Student A.

Personal Best Think of a person that you know well. Imagine what he/she has in his/her man bag or handbag. Say the objects.

1 SKILLS SPEAKING — asking for and giving personal information ■ asking for clarification

1D Where's my wallet?

1 Answer the questions below.
1. Look at the picture of a lost property office. What can you see?
2. What other things can you find in a lost property office?
3. What things do you often lose?
4. What buildings usually have a lost property office?

2 A ▶ 1.16 Watch or listen to the first part of a webshow called *Learning Curve*. What object is missing?

B ▶ 1.16 Watch or listen again. Tick (✓) the things that are in Kate's backpack.

keys ☐	sunglasses ☐	biscuits ☐
wallet ☐	mirror ☐	tissues ☐
stamps ☐	tablet ☐	chewing gum ☐

3 ▶ 1.17 Watch or listen to the second part of the show. Are the sentences true (T) or false (F)?
1. The assistant in the lost property office is called Harry. ____
2. Kate's personal information is already in the computer. ____
3. Kate loves James Bond. ____
4. Kate's phone is in the assistant's box. ____
5. Simon's phone is different from Kate's. ____

4 A In pairs, complete the questions in the conversation with the words in the box.

> address   mobile number   email address   postcode   number   first name   spell

Assistant	Here's the lost property form. Time to fill it out. I'm ready. What's your ¹_____?	**Kate**	It's 02079 46007.
Kate	It's Kate.	**Simon**	Isn't that your home phone number?
Assistant	K-A-T-E. What's your surname?	**Kate**	Yes, he can call me at home!
Kate	Oh ... it's McRea.	**Assistant**	Could you say that again, please?
Assistant	How do you ²_____ that, please?	**Kate**	Yes, it's 02079 46007.
Kate	M-C-R-E-A.	**Assistant**	And what's your ⁵_____, please?
Assistant	Thanks. And what's your ³_____?	**Kate**	222 Baker Street, Marylebone, London.
Kate	It's missing.	**Assistant**	OK. What's your ⁶_____?
Assistant	Could you say that again, please?	**Kate**	NW1 5RT.
Kate	My cell phone is lost.	**Assistant**	Do you have an ⁷_____?
Assistant	OK. Lost mobile. What's your ⁴_____, please?	**Kate**	Yes, it's k.mcrea_007@gmail.com.

B ▶ 1.17 Watch or listen again to check.

10

asking for and giving personal information ■ asking for clarification   **SPEAKING**   **SKILLS**   **1D**

Conversation builder — asking for and giving personal information

Asking for information:
What's your first name/surname/ address/mobile number/(home phone) number?
Do you have an email address?
How do you spell that, please?

Saying your phone number:
02079 46007 – oh two oh seven nine four six double oh seven

Saying your email address:
k.mcrea_007@gmail.com – k dot mcrea underscore double oh seven at g mail dot com

5 Read the Conversation builder. Answer the questions in pairs.
1 How do you say '0' and '44' in a phone number?
2 How do you say '@', '_' and '.com' in an email address?

6 ▶ 1.17 Read the sentences. Then watch or listen again. Choose the correct options to complete the sentences.
1 The assistant asks Kate to spell her *first name / surname / address*.
2 He asks her to say her *postcode / email address / home phone number* again.

Skill — asking for clarification

When you don't understand something, ask the speaker for help:
- Ask him/her to say the sentence again or to spell the word.
- Use **Sorry, could you ...** and **please** to be polite:
  Sorry, could you say that again, please?   How do you spell that, please?
- Use polite intonation: Sorry, could you say that again, please?

7 ▶ 1.18 Read the Skill box. Listen and repeat the questions when you hear the beeps. Copy the intonation.

8 ▶ 1.19 Listen to three conversations in a school lost property office. For what information does the assistant ask for clarification?

Conversation 1   address / postcode / email address
Conversation 2   home phone number / mobile number / postcode
Conversation 3   first name / surname / first name and surname

Go to Communication practice: Student A page 158, Student B page 167

9 A PREPARE You lose an important personal object. Look at the Conversation builder again. Think about your answers to the questions.

B PRACTISE You are at the lost property office. In pairs, take turns to ask and answer questions and complete the form for your partner. Ask for clarification to check the information is correct.

First name	Email address
Surname	Mobile number
Address	Home phone number
Postcode	

C PERSONAL BEST Swap your form with your partner. Read his/her work and correct any mistakes. How could you improve it?

Personal Best   Write the email addresses and phone numbers of five people you know. Practise saying them in English.

11

UNIT 2 Work and play

LANGUAGE present simple: positive and negative ■ jobs and job verbs

2A What I do

1 Look at the pictures. What jobs can you see?

2 A Read the text. Check your answers to exercise 1.

B Label the pictures with the names of the people. What other jobs are mentioned in the text?

My other job

Lots of people around the world have two jobs. Sometimes it's because they need the money and sometimes they want to learn something new. Let's meet some people who each have two jobs.

1 I'm Luisa. I'm from Brazil, but I live in Lisbon with my parents and my sister. I work as a receptionist for an IT company in an office in the city centre, but I also help my parents in our family restaurant in the evening and at the weekend. It's a traditional Brazilian restaurant. My sister helps, too. My parents cook the food and we serve it! I like my two jobs, but I don't have a lot of free time.

2 Michal lives in Prague. He's a mechanic and he works in a garage. He likes his job because he loves cars, but he doesn't work there at the weekend. On Saturdays, he has a second job – he's a tour guide for tourists. He knows a lot about his city.

3 Zoe's 26 years old and lives in Manchester in the UK. She's a receptionist for a TV company. She works from 9 a.m. to 5 p.m. during the week. Zoe has another job three evenings a week – she teaches Zumba in a gym. She doesn't work at the weekend.

4 Isaac's from Jamaica, but he lives in New York. He's a taxi driver and he works every day. Isaac likes his job and he loves New York. He often goes back to Jamaica for his other job. He doesn't drive a taxi in Jamaica – he's a singer and he sings at festivals!

3 Read the text again. Write the names of the people.
  1 They work with cars. _____, _____
  2 He/She works with food. _____
  3 They have office jobs. _____, _____
  4 They come from one country and work in another country. _____, _____
  5 They work at the weekend. _____, _____, _____

4 Complete the sentences with verbs from the text.
  1 I _____ in Lisbon.
  2 My sister _____, too.
  3 My parents _____ the food.
  4 I _____ a lot of free time.
  5 She _____ Zumba in a gym.
  6 He _____ a taxi in Jamaica.

Go to Vocabulary practice: jobs and job verbs, page 138

12

present simple: positive and negative ■ jobs and job verbs   **LANGUAGE**   **2A**

5 Complete the rules for the present simple. Use the text to help you. Then read the Grammar box.
1 For the *he/she/it* form, we add _____ or _____ to the infinitive form of the verb.
2 For the negative form, we use _____ and _____.

> **Grammar** present simple: positive and negative
>
> Positive:
> I **work** for an IT company.   He **loves** New York.   She **teaches** Zumba.   My parents **cook** the food.
> Negative:
> I **don't have** a lot of free time.   He **doesn't drive** a taxi.

Go to Grammar practice: present simple: positive and negative, page 114

6 Complete the text with the correct form of the verbs in brackets in the present simple.

My parents ¹_____ (have) a hotel in a small town in Spain. I ²_____ (go) to college every day, but I ³_____ (help) my parents in the evening. My dad ⁴_____ (cook) the food, but he ⁵_____ (not serve) it – that's my job. I have two sisters, but they ⁶_____ (not work) in the restaurant. One sister ⁷_____ (live) in Germany and my other sister ⁸_____ (work) in a hospital.

7 A ▶2.4 **Pronunciation:** -s and -es endings Listen and repeat the sounds and verbs in the table.

/s/	/z/	/ɪz/
likes	goes	finishes

B ▶2.5 Add the verbs to the table. Listen and check.

teaches   lives   helps   works   drives   watches   makes   sells

8 ▶2.6 In pairs, say the sentences. Listen, check and repeat.
1 He teaches English.
2 He lives in New York.
3 She helps her parents.
4 He works from 2 p.m. to 10 p.m. every day.
5 He drives a taxi.
6 She watches TV after work.
7 She makes clothes in a factory.
8 She sells books in a shop.

9 A Think of three people you know. Write about their jobs, but don't say what the jobs are.

My friend Ana works in the city. She doesn't work at the weekend. She likes her job because she works with people. She cuts people's hair.

B In pairs, tell each other about your people. Guess the jobs.
A *Is Ana a hairdresser?*   **B** *Yes, she is. Your turn.*

Go to Communication practice: Student A page 159, Student B page 168

10 A Write about your job. Use the prompts to help you.

(I'm a …)   (I work in/for a …)   (In my job, I …)   (I work in the week/ at the weekend.)   (I work/don't work in the evening.)   (I like/don't like my job because …)

B Work in groups of five or six. Swap your descriptions with another student. Take turns to talk about the person whose description you have. The other students guess who it is.
A *This person's a teacher. She works in a language school. She teaches Spanish. She likes her job. She works in the evening, but she doesn't work at the weekend.*
B *I think Carla's a teacher. Carla, is it you?*

Personal **Best**   Write sentences about a dream job.   13

2 SKILLS LISTENING listening for names, places, days and times ■ activities (1)

2B Weekdays, weekends

1 Match the activities in the box with pictures a–h.

> play tennis   read a book   go to the cinema   watch TV
> go for a walk   listen to music   study   meet friends

2 In pairs, talk about the activities in exercise 1. What activities do you do?

I listen to music in the car. I don't go to the cinema.

Go to Vocabulary practice: activities (1), page 139

3 ▶ 2.8 Watch or listen to the first part of *Learning Curve*. What do they talk about? Tick (✓) the two correct answers.

a free-time activities and jobs ☐
b free-time activities ☐
c people who don't have any free time ☐

Skill listening for names, places, days and times

Names, places, days and times are important pieces of information when you listen.
- Important words like names, places, days and times are usually stressed. Listen for stressed words.
- We often use prepositions with places, days and times: *in France*, *on Monday*, *at 6.30*, etc. Listen for the prepositions *in*, *on* and *at*.
- Remember to use capital letters for names, places and days when you write them down.

4 A ▶ 2.8 Read the Skill box. Watch or listen again. Complete the table with words from the box.

> lawyer   Argentinian   dance teacher   Puerto Rican
> Marcus   English   Maggie   Pablo   tennis coach

Name	Nationality	Job

B In pairs, talk about people you know. Do they love their jobs? Why?/Why not?

My friend Justyna's Polish. She's a receptionist. She likes her job, but she doesn't love it.

listening for names, places, days and times ■ activities (1) **LISTENING** **SKILLS** **2B**

5 ▶ 2.9 Watch or listen to the second part of the show. Complete the sentences with the names and cities in the box.

Toronto   Chip   New York   Gillian   Khan   London

1 This is _____.
   She's from _____.

2 This is _____.
   He lives in _____.

3 This is _____.
   He's from _____.

6 ▶ 2.9 Watch or listen again. Are the sentences true (T) or false (F)?
1 Gillian meets friends on Saturday. ____
2 She goes for a run on Monday mornings. ____
3 Khan watches football on Saturday evenings. ____
4 He studies Italian and Spanish. ____
5 Chip starts work at 9 a.m. every day. ____
6 He finishes work at 4 p.m. ____

7 In pairs, talk about the people in the video. Answer the questions.
1 Where do they work?
2 What activities do they do in their free time?
3 What do you think of their jobs?
4 Do you do the same activities in your free time?

Listening builder   introduction to the sound /ə/

The unstressed vowel sound /ə/ is also called 'schwa'. It is very common in English. We use it in almost every sentence. It is underlined in these phrases:
Marc<u>us</u> isn't <u>a</u> fam<u>ous</u> tennis play<u>er</u>.   What <u>do</u> you do in y<u>our</u> free time?   We want <u>to</u> know!

8 ▶ 2.10 Read the Listening builder. Read the sentences and underline the letters that you think have the sound /ə/. Then listen and check.
1 My sister's a doctor.
2 When do you play tennis?
3 I relax at the weekend.
4 John's a police officer.
5 I want to go out for dinner.

9 **A** Think of three people that you know. Make notes about the following questions:
• Where do they live? What's their job?
• What activities do they do in their free time? When do they do them?
my friend Victoria – London – studies French – Wednesday evenings

B Take turns to tell your partner about the people. Listen and complete the chart about your partner's people.

Name	Place	Activity	Day(s)/Time

Personal Best   What do you remember about the people in the video? Write a sentence about each person.

15

2 LANGUAGE present simple: questions

2C Find a flatmate

1 Look at the pictures in the text. What do you think 'speed-flatmating' is?

2 A Read the text and check your answer to exercise 1.

B Look at the questions. Who asks them: people who need a flatmate or people who need a room in a flat, or both?

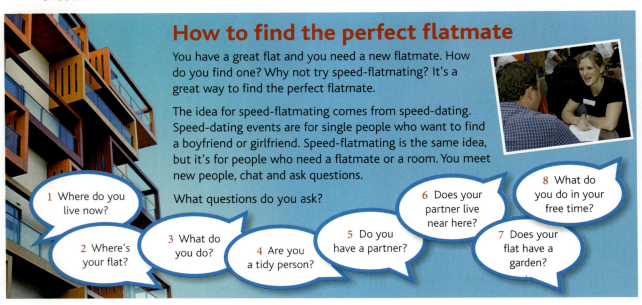

How to find the perfect flatmate

You have a great flat and you need a new flatmate. How do you find one? Why not try speed-flatmating? It's a great way to find the perfect flatmate.

The idea for speed-flatmating comes from speed-dating. Speed-dating events are for single people who want to find a boyfriend or girlfriend. Speed-flatmating is the same idea, but it's for people who need a flatmate or a room. You meet new people, chat and ask questions.

What questions do you ask?

1 Where do you live now?
2 Where's your flat?
3 What do you do?
4 Are you a tidy person?
5 Do you have a partner?
6 Does your partner live near here?
7 Does your flat have a garden?
8 What do you do in your free time?

3 A ▶ 2.11 Bruce is at a speed-flatmating event. He is looking for a flatmate. Listen and decide who is the best flatmate for Bruce – Mike, Phil or Andrea. Why?

B ▶ 2.11 Listen again. Are the sentences true (T) or false (F)?

1 Mike and Bruce work at the weekend. ____
2 Bruce is a DJ in a club. ____
3 Phil doesn't work near Bruce's flat. ____
4 Phil doesn't like his job. ____
5 Andrea doesn't live with her parents. ____
6 Bruce has a partner. ____

4 Match questions 1–5 with answers a–e.

1 Where do you work?
2 What do you do?
3 Do you work in the evening?
4 Where does your partner live?
5 Do you have a partner?

a He lives in another city.
b I work in a local restaurant.
c No, I don't. Not at the moment.
d I'm an accountant.
e Yes, I do. I finish at about 11.30.

5 A Look at the questions in exercise 4. Which questions have a *yes/no* answer?

B Complete the rule. Then read the Grammar box.
We use the auxiliary verbs ¹_____ and ²_____ to make questions in the present simple.

Grammar present simple: questions

yes/no questions and short answers:
Do you **work** long hours?   Yes, I do.   No, I don't.
Does she **go** out?   Yes, she does.   No, she doesn't.

Wh- questions:
What **do** you **do** in your free time?
Where **do** you **work**?
When **does** he **finish**?

Look! We don't use *do* and *don't* in questions with the verb *be*:
Do you **live** in Oxford?   **Are** you from Oxford?

Go to Grammar practice: present simple: questions, page 115

present simple: questions LANGUAGE 2C

6 A ▶ 2.13 **Pronunciation:** auxiliary verbs *do* and *does* in questions Listen to the questions. How do we pronounce *do* and *does*?

1 Do you listen to music?
2 Does Phil have a cat?
3 When do you finish work?
4 What does Bruce do after work?
5 Where do they live?
6 Do they play tennis?

B ▶ 2.13 Listen again and underline the stressed words. Repeat the questions.

7 A Complete the questions asked by different people at a speed-flatmating event.

1 _____ you like music?
2 _____ your flat have two bathrooms?
3 What kind of TV programmes _____ you watch?
4 Where _____ you work?
5 Who _____ you live with at the moment?
6 _____ you go out in the evening?

B Ask and answer the questions in pairs.

8 A Do the quiz in pairs. Write down your partner's answers.

B Are you and your partner similar?

What type of **flatmate are you?**

1 What time / you / go to bed?
  a 9.00-11.00 b 11.00-01.00 c after 1.00
2 What / you / have for dinner?
  a I cook a healthy meal. b I have a pizza on the sofa. c I go out for dinner.
3 What / do / at the weekend?
  a I relax at home. b I spend time with friends. c I go to parties.
4 How many friends / you / have?
  a 4 or 5 good friends b about 50 c more than 500 on Facebook
5 Which / be / your perfect job?
  a a writer b a fashion designer c a rock singer

9 A What do you do in your free time? Ask and answer questions in pairs.

  A *What do you do in your free time?*   B *I meet friends, I go for a coffee, I spend time with my family.*

B Work with a new partner. Ask and answer questions about your first partner.

What does Gabriela do in her free time?

Go to Communication practice: Student A page 159, Student B page 168

10 A Imagine that you want to find a flatmate. Write six questions to ask people.

B Go speed-flatmating with your classmates. Talk to lots of people. Ask and answer questions. Choose three good flatmates.

  A *Who do you live with at the moment?*
  B *I live in a flat with three other people.*

Personal Best Imagine you meet someone at speed-flatmating who is a terrible flatmate. Write the conversation you have with him/her.

2 SKILLS WRITING opening and closing an informal email ■ connectors: *and*, *but* and *or*

2D A new city

1 Think about a town or city that you know well. What do you do there? In pairs, say three sentences to describe the place.

I like Rio de Janeiro. It's a great city. I eat out with my family, I go to the beach and I go to clubs with my friends.

2 Pieter is in a new city. Read his email to Hayley. Why is he writing? Choose the correct answer.
 a to tell her about his new life
 b to tell her about his new girlfriend
 c to invite her to visit

Hi Hayley,

How are things back home in Australia?

I'm fine here in Singapore. I love life here – it's a fantastic city for students! I share a flat with two more students near the university. My flatmates are called Steve and Susie, and they're great!

I have a part-time job. I work in an Italian restaurant as a waiter. Susie has a job there, too, but I don't work with her because she works on different days. Steve doesn't have a job at the moment because he goes to university every day.

In the evenings, I study or I relax and watch TV. I don't have much free time, but sometimes I go to the cinema with Steve and Susie. At the weekends, I do sport or I go out with my friends. I love the nightclubs in Singapore!

Write soon with your news.

Pieter

3 Read the email again and answer the questions.
 1 Where is Pieter from?
 2 Who does he live with?
 3 What does he do in Singapore in his free time?
 4 What do Pieter and his friends do when they go out?
 5 Where does Susie work?
 6 Why doesn't Steve work?

🔧 Skill opening and closing an informal email

We write informal emails to people we know well, like friends and family.

Opening: Closing:
Hi/Hello (+ name)   *Hey!*   *Hello!*   *Write soon (with your news).*   *Take care.*   *See you soon.*

For very close friends and family, we often close with *Love* + (your name) or (your name) + *xx*.

4 Read the Skill box. Which opening and closing words or phrases does Pieter use?

18

opening and closing an informal email ■ connectors: *and*, *but* and *or* **WRITING** **SKILLS** **2D**

5 Complete the emails with opening and closing phrases.

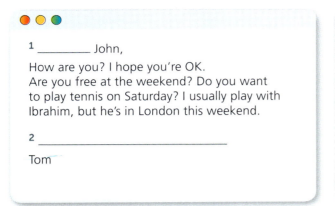

1 _____ John,
How are you? I hope you're OK.
Are you free at the weekend? Do you want to play tennis on Saturday? I usually play with Ibrahim, but he's in London this weekend.

2 _____

Tom

3 _____ Sara!
How are you? How's your new job?
I'm in a new flat and I have two new flatmates! The flat's lovely and my flatmates are really nice. Do you want to see a film or go for a coffee at the weekend? I want to hear your news!

4 _____

Nikki xx

> **Text builder** connectors: *and*, *but* and *or*
>
> We use *and* to add information:
> *My flatmates are called Steve and Susie,* **and** *they're great!*
>
> We use *but* to introduce a different idea:
> *I don't have much free time,* **but** *sometimes I go to the cinema.*
>
> We use *or* to add another possibility:
> *In the evenings, I study* **or** *I relax and watch TV.*

6 Read the Text builder. Find other examples of connectors in Pieter's email.

7 Complete the sentences with *and*, *but* and *or*.
1 Gianpiero's my flatmate _____ he's 22 years old.
2 I like my job, _____ I don't like my boss.
3 At the weekend, I meet my parents at a restaurant _____ I go to their house for lunch.
4 I play the guitar, _____ I'm not in a band.
5 I have two jobs. I work in a café _____ I drive a taxi.
6 Does your girlfriend have a job _____ is she a student?

8 Complete the sentences with your own ideas.
1 Elena's from Argentina and she ...
2 Stefan's from Germany, but he ...
3 We often go out at the weekend and we ...
4 In the evenings, we go to the cinema or we ...
5 I watch football on TV, but I don't watch ...
6 In the evening, I ... or I ...

9 A PREPARE Plan an email about your life for a friend in another city. Answer the questions.
• Where do you live?
• Who do you live with? Do you like him/her/them?
• Do you have a job? What do you do?
• What do you do in your free time at home? What do you do when you go out?

B PRACTISE Write the email. Use different paragraphs to write about your home, your job and your free time. Use *and*, *but* and *or* to connect your ideas.
• Open your email.
• Paragraph 1: Say where you live and who you live with.
• Paragraph 2: Say if you have a job and describe what you do.
• Paragraph 3: Describe what you do in your free time.
• Close your email.

C PERSONAL BEST Swap emails with a partner. Underline three sentences with connectors that you think are interesting.

Personal Best — Describe a city in a different country. Ask your partner to guess the city.

19

1 and 2 REVIEW and PRACTICE

Grammar

1 Choose the correct options to complete the sentences.

1 _____ in Paris.
 a My brother works
 b My brother work
 c My brother has

2 My sister _____ .
 a lives with his parents
 b lives with our parents
 c lives with their parents

3 _____ at the weekend?
 a What does you do
 b What you do
 c What do you do

4 Jack _____ . He's an electrician.
 a isn't builder
 b isn't a builder
 c no build

5 How old are you? _____ 25.
 a I
 b I've
 c I'm

6 My hairdresser's Italian. _____ .
 a She comes from Rome
 b They come from Rome
 c She come from Rome

7 _____ English?
 a Your wife's
 b Has your wife
 c Is your wife

8 Who _____ ?
 a do work for
 b do you work for
 c does he works for

2 Put the words in the correct order.

1 flat London Harry in Tim and live a in
 _____

2 Ireland from 's Harry
 _____

3 a American Tim in 's and bank works
 _____

4 nine He at starts work
 _____

5 restaurant works Harry a in
 _____

6 watch after TV work They
 _____

7 with out At friends the they go weekend
 _____

8 listen and computer games play They music to
 _____

3 Complete the text with the correct form of the verbs in brackets.

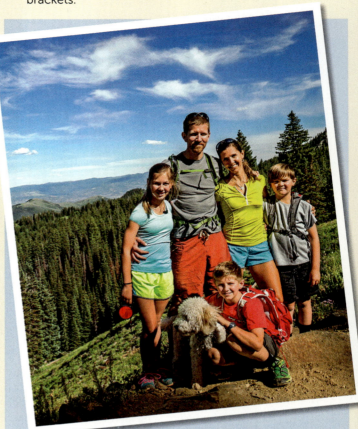

Charles [1] _____ (live) in France, but he works in Switzerland. His wife's Swedish and they [2] _____ (have) three children. He [3] _____ (be) a lawyer and she [4] _____ (teach) music. In the evening, she [5] _____ (play) the guitar and he [6] _____ (repair) watches. At the weekend, they [7] _____ (meet) friends or [8] _____ (relax) with the family.

Vocabulary

1 Circle the word that is different. Explain your answer.

1 guitar	newspaper	tennis	games
2 doctor	dentist	teach	lawyer
3 France	Irish	Germany	Italy
4 police officer	Argentinian	nurse	teacher
5 Mexican	French	Japan	Italian
6 handbag	wallet	gloves	keys
7 sixty	nineteen	seventy	eighty
8 chef	wear	repair	serve

20

REVIEW and PRACTICE — 1 and 2

2 Match the definitions 1–8 with the objects a–h.
1 They help you see better.
2 They keep your hands warm.
3 It helps you see at night.
4 You keep your money in it.
5 It tells you the time.
6 You use it to send a letter.
7 You use them to open and close a door.
8 You use this on your hair.

a torch
b stamp
c glasses
d wallet
e watch
f comb
g keys
h gloves

3 Complete the sentences with the jobs in the box.

chef   dentist   flight attendant   nurse
waiter   mechanic   hairdresser   teacher

1 A _____ serves food in a restaurant.
2 My cousin's a _____ with American Airlines.
3 A _____ cooks the food in a restaurant.
4 A _____ works in a garage and repairs cars.
5 A _____ cuts hair.
6 If you have problems with your teeth, see a _____ .
7 My _____ helps me with my English.
8 My sister's a _____ . She works in a hospital in London.

4 Put the words in the correct columns.

accountant   gloves   France   Turkish   glasses
sunglasses   Mexican   American   doctor   lawyer
UK   taxi driver   Japan   Irish   tissues   Italy

Jobs	Countries	Nationalities	Objects

Personal Best

Lesson 1A — Name five nationalities.

Lesson 2A — Name five jobs.

Lesson 1A — Write two sentences about yourself using the verb *be*: one positive, one negative.

Lesson 2A — Write three sentences about your friends using the present simple.

Lesson 1B — Write three simple statements with *be*.

Lesson 2C — Write a *yes/no* question using *do* or *does*.

Lesson 1C — Name five things in your bag.

Lesson 2C — Write three questions you can ask the first time you meet someone.

Lesson 1C — Write three sentences using *his*, *her* and *their*.

Lesson 2D — Give two expressions for closing an informal email.

Lesson 1D — Give two expressions to ask for clarification.

Lesson 2D — Write one sentence with *but* and one with *or*.

21

UNIT 3

People in my life

LANGUAGE adverbs and expressions of frequency ■ family

3A Time together

1 When and where do you spend time with your family? Tell your partner.
I see my family at the weekend. We have lunch together on Sundays.

2 Look at the pictures of different family activities. How many generations can you see? What are they doing together?

3 **A** Read the text. Complete it with the verbs in the box.

go   cook   make   see   play   watch

Family get-togethers

Once a year, my whole family meet at my parents' house for a weekend of fun, music and great food. We're a big family and there are three generations of us!

In the morning, we often ¹_____ games with the children in the park. My brother Ben has a boy and a girl. My niece and nephew are crazy about football, so we usually play that.

In the afternoon, we ²_____ for a walk or stay at home. We sit in the garden and we sometimes ³_____ things with the children. My sister-in-law Lois teaches five-year-olds and she always brings lots of paper and pens.

In the evening, we ⁴_____ dinner. Food's always an important part of the weekend! Our food's very international – my grandmother's Portuguese, my sister-in-law's American and my husband's Polish. We often have Mexican food because we all love it.

We never ⁵_____ television – we prefer to chat together. My Uncle Paul and my cousins Joe and Megan play music. Uncle Paul and Joe play the guitar, and Megan sings and plays the piano. They're really good.

I don't often ⁶_____ my family because we all live in different parts of the country, but I love these weekends. They're really special.

B ▶ 3.1 Listen and check your answers.

4 **A** Read the text again and choose the correct options.
1 The writer is Ben's *sister / aunt*.
2 Lois is Ben's *sister / wife*.
3 Paul is Joe's *father / grandfather*.
4 Megan is Paul's *son / daughter*.

B Look at the main picture in the text. What relation to the writer do you think the people are?

Go to Vocabulary practice: family, page 140

22

adverbs and expressions of frequency ■ family   **LANGUAGE**   **3A**

5 ▶ 3.4 Listen to Ben and match the activities with the people and the expressions of frequency.

1 play tennis   son   every day
2 read stories   grandmother   once a week
3 go for a coffee   son and daughter   once a month
4 watch TV   cousin   three times a week
5 go out for dinner   wife   every evening
6 buy food   brother-in-law   twice a month

6 A Underline the adverbs of frequency in the text on page 22. Complete the rule.

Adverbs of frequency go *before / after* the verb *be* and *before / after* other verbs.

B Look at the expressions of frequency in exercise 5. Which word means 'one time'? Which word means 'two times'? Then read the Grammar box.

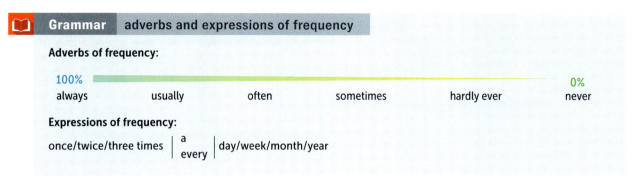

Grammar adverbs and expressions of frequency

Adverbs of frequency:

100% ── 0%
always   usually   often   sometimes   hardly ever   never

Expressions of frequency:

once/twice/three times | a / every | day/week/month/year

Go to Grammar practice: adverbs and expressions of frequency, page 116

7 A ▶ 3.6 **Pronunciation:** sentence stress   Listen to the sentences. Underline the stressed words or syllables. Are the adverbs and expressions of frequency stressed?

1 I sometimes play the guitar.
2 He's often late.
3 We never have a takeaway.
4 They eat out once a week.
5 She sees her grandparents three times a year.
6 I listen to the radio every day.

B ▶ 3.6 Listen again and repeat the sentences. Copy the rhythm.

8 A Write five sentences about you and your family. Use different frequency adverbs and expressions.

I often go for a coffee with my mother-in-law.   *I sometimes watch TV with my grandparents.*
I play football with my brother once a week.

B In pairs, say your sentences. Do you do the same activities with the same people?

Go to Communication practice: Student A page 159, Student B page 168

9 A Ask and answer questions with your classmates about how frequently you do the activities.

go to (the cinema)   play (a sport)   cook   meet (your cousins)   drive a car   go for a run

A *How often do you go to the cinema?*   B *Once a month. What about you?*   A *I never go to the cinema.*

B Complete the sentences about your classmates.

1 _____ never goes _____.
2 _____ sometimes plays _____.
3 _____ cooks _____.
4 _____ meets his/her _____.
5 _____ drives a car _____.
6 _____ goes for a run _____.

Personal **Best**   Draw your family tree. Choose five people in your family and write a sentence about each of them.   23

3 SKILLS READING scanning a text ■ *also* and *too*

3B A new group

1 Look at the picture. In pairs, talk about how you usually meet new people in your town or city.

> **Skill** scanning a text
>
> Scanning means reading quickly to find specific information; for example, you scan a TV guide for a programme or a timetable for a train's arrival time. You don't read everything. You only look for the information you want.

2 A Read the Skill box. Imagine that you like art and photography. Scan the website to find groups that are suitable for you.

B You are free on Monday and Wednesday evenings. Which art or photography group can you join? Scan the website again.

3 Read the website again and read for detail. Are the sentences true (T) or false (F)?

1 The Walking Group meets at the weekend. ____
2 The Drawing Club always meets in a studio. ____
3 The Italian Group sometimes goes to Italy. ____
4 The Camera Club has an exhibition once a year. ____
5 In the International Friends Group, people cook in their homes every week. ____
6 Children and young people watch the Drama Group's shows. ____
7 The Cooking Club meets once a week. ____
8 The Film Group always meets every Saturday evening. ____

> **Text builder** *also* and *too*
>
> *Also* and *too* are adverbs that we use to add extra information. *Also* usually goes after the verb *be* and before other verbs. *Too* usually goes at the end of the sentence.

4 A Read the Text builder. <u>Underline</u> examples of *also* and *too* on the website.

B Choose the correct words to complete the sentences.
1 She plays the guitar and she *also / too* writes stories.
2 I want to join the Camera Club and the Cooking Club, *also / too*.
3 We go to the cinema once a month and we sometimes go to the theatre, *also / too*.
4 They go to a restaurant twice a week and they *also / too* have a takeaway once a week.

5 In pairs, discuss which group on the website you like most. Why?

6 A Plan a new group for the website. Think about the following:
What does it do? How often does it meet? Where does it meet?

B Tell the class about your new group and listen to your classmates' groups. Decide which new group you like most.

scanning a text ■ *also* and *too* READING **SKILLS** **3B**

Clubs and groups near you

WALKING GROUP

We're a walking club for people who love the countryside. We go for lots of walks of different lengths and levels of difficulty. We start at 9.30 a.m. on Sunday mornings and we usually finish at about 5 p.m.

INTERNATIONAL FRIENDS GROUP

We're a friendly group who meet every week on Tuesdays. We usually meet in a restaurant and we often go to the cinema and theatre. We want to learn about other countries and cultures, and have a good time, too!

DRAWING CLUB

This is a club for art lovers of all ages. Beginners are very welcome! We don't have a teacher, but we all learn from each other. We work in a studio on Thursday evenings and we also go outside to draw once a month.

DRAMA GROUP
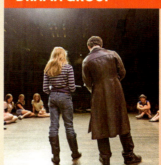
We're a big group, but we always welcome new members. We perform three shows a year at the local arts centre and at local schools, too. We meet on Wednesday evenings at 7.30.

ITALIAN GROUP

Buongiorno! We're a group of people who speak Italian and who are interested in Italian culture. We meet at an Italian restaurant once a month, on a Friday evening. We also watch Italian films together.

COOKING CLUB

We meet every Saturday to cook together in someone's home and then enjoy a great meal! We try lots of new and delicious food and we also meet other people who love cooking.

CAMERA CLUB

Do you like photography? If so, come and join our camera club! We meet every Monday at 7 p.m. We have talks and discussions about different kinds of photography and we show each other our own photos.

FILM GROUP

We don't have a regular meeting! Members post a message on the website and invite others to join them for a film. After watching the film, we usually have a coffee and chat. It's a great way to enjoy films and make new friends, too.

Personal Best Describe a group that you're in now or when you were a child.

3 LANGUAGE — love, like, hate, enjoy, don't mind + noun/-ing form ■ activities (2)

3C Opposites attract

1 Which activities are good for a couple to do together? In pairs, choose five activities and explain why.

> going on holiday   visiting relatives   doing sport   going cycling   playing computer games
> visiting museums   relaxing at home   studying

Go to Vocabulary practice: activities (2), page 141

2 A Read the text about Cara and Chris. What do they do together?

B Discuss the questions in pairs.
1 Are Cara and Chris happy that they are very different? Why/Why not?
2 Do you think opposites attract?

Do opposites really attract? Or is it better to find someone similar to you? We ask one couple why they are together when they are so different from each other.

OPPOSITES attract

CARA

My boyfriend Chris and I are very different. He's always out and he loves doing sport. He likes running and he loves playing tennis. I don't mind tennis, but I hate running! I like different activities: I enjoy doing yoga in the park and I love reading. But I think we're a great couple. Why? We both like living in the city. We enjoy good restaurants and we love meeting our friends at the weekend, but I sometimes prefer to spend a quiet evening with him at home.

CHRIS

I think it's great that Cara and I have our own interests. I enjoy being active: I play tennis and go running every day. Cara enjoys relaxing at home and she loves visiting museums and galleries. I don't mind visiting museums, but I hate art! We do some things together – we both love going bowling, for example, but I don't want a girlfriend who's just like me. They say 'opposites attract' and I agree!

3 A Work in pairs. Read the text again. Student A: write about Cara. Student B: write about Chris. Complete the sentences.

Student A
1 Cara loves _____.
2 She enjoys _____.
3 She likes _____.
4 She doesn't mind _____.
5 She hates _____.

Student B
1 Chris loves _____.
2 He enjoys _____.
3 He likes _____.
4 He doesn't mind _____.
5 He hates _____.

B ▶ 3.8 Tell your partner your answers. Listen and check.

love, *like*, *hate*, *enjoy*, *don't mind* + noun/*-ing* form ■ activities (2) | LANGUAGE | **3C**

4 Look at the sentences in exercise 3. Choose the correct option to complete the rule. Then read the Grammar box.

After *love*, *like*, *hate*, *enjoy* and *don't mind* we usually use
a a noun or *-ing* form.
b *to* + infinitive.

> **Grammar** *love*, *like*, *hate*, *enjoy*, *don't mind* + noun/*-ing* form
>
> *love*, *like*, etc. + noun:
> I **love** TV.
> I **like** books.
> I **enjoy** music.
> I **don't mind** tennis.
> I **hate** museums.
>
> *love*, *like*, etc. + *-ing* form of verb:
> I **love watching** TV.
> I **like reading** books.
> I **enjoy listening** to music.
> I **don't mind playing** tennis.
> I **hate visiting** museums.

Go to Grammar practice: *love, like, hate, enjoy, don't mind* + noun/*-ing* form, page 117

5 A ▶ 3.10 **Pronunciation:** *-ing* forms. Listen and repeat the verbs.
watching   reading   visiting   doing   going   being   playing   running

B ▶ 3.11 Say the sentences. Listen, check and repeat.
1 I don't mind visiting museums.
2 She doesn't like going bowling.
3 I love reading magazines.
4 He hates going to the gym.
5 We enjoy doing yoga.

6 A Complete Stephanie's profile with the correct form of the verbs in the box.

do   talk   watch   cook   be   play

About me:
Stephanie Ellis

In the evening, I usually make dinner because I don't mind ¹_____. After dinner, I walk my dog Bruno for an hour. It's very relaxing and I enjoy ²_____ to other dog walkers. I love ³_____ exercise and sometimes I go running with a friend. I also love ⁴_____ at home with Bruno, but I don't like ⁵_____ TV and I hate ⁶_____ computer games.

B Look again at the text on page 26. Who do you think is Stephanie's friend: Cara or Chris?

Go to Communication practice: Student A page 159, Student B page 168

7 A Write two true sentences for you for each verb. Use nouns and *-ing* forms.
- I love …
- I like …
- I enjoy …
- I don't mind …
- I don't like …
- I hate …

B Compare your sentences with a partner. Are you similar or different?

A *I enjoy swimming in the sea.*   B *I don't like swimming. I enjoy …*

Personal Best Choose someone you know. Write about what he/she loves, likes and hates doing.

3 SKILLS SPEAKING making arrangements ■ accepting or declining an invitation

3D A night out

1 A Look at the clocks. Match them with the times.

1 It's half past ten. ____
2 It's quarter past ten. ____
3 It's ten o'clock. ____
4 It's twenty-five past ten. ____
5 It's seven minutes past ten. ____
6 It's quarter to eleven. ____
7 It's five past ten. ____
8 It's twenty past ten. ____
9 It's twenty-five to eleven. ____
10 It's ten to eleven. ____

B ▶ 3.12 Listen and check. Listen again and repeat.

2 ▶ 3.13 Watch or listen to the first part of *Learning Curve*. What's Penny's main problem?

a She is late.
b Ethan is late.
c They don't know what time it is.

3 ▶ 3.13 Watch or listen again. Choose the correct times.

1 Penny's watch says it's five minutes *to/past* ten.
2 The clock on the wall says it's *seven/eleven* minutes past ten.
3 The clock on Penny's computer says it's *quarter past/half past* ten.
4 Ethan wants to meet Penny at *ten to/ten past* eleven.
5 Ethan's phone says it's ten *thirty/forty*.

4 ▶ 3.14 Watch or listen to the second part of the show and answer the questions.

1 What two activities do they all want to do?
2 What time does Penny arrange to meet Taylor and Ethan?

making arrangements ■ accepting or declining an invitation   SPEAKING   SKILLS   3D

Conversation builder — making arrangements

Suggesting an activity:
Would you like to …?   Do you want to …?   How about having dinner/How about we have dinner …?
Let's go together.   Do you have plans after …?   Are you free for lunch on Thursday?

Agreeing a time:
What time is good for you?   Let's say 8.00 p.m.   How about we meet tomorrow at six?
About seven?   Can we go at 8 p.m.?

5 A ▶ 3.14 Read the Conversation builder. Match the halves to make complete sentences. Watch or listen again and check.

1 What time is   a at five thirty in front of our building?
2 How about we meet   b to come?
3 Do you want to   c seven o'clock?
4 Would you like   d good for you?
5 Are you both free   e for dinner?
6 Can we go at   f go bowling tonight?

B Who says questions 1–6? Write M (Marc), E (Ethan), T (Taylor) or P (Penny). Watch or listen again to check if necessary.

1 ____   3 ____   5 ____
2 ____   4 ____   6 ____

6 In pairs, make arrangements to see a film and go shopping together. Take turns to suggest the activity.

Skill — accepting or declining an invitation

When you accept or decline an invitation, it's important to be polite.
- When you accept, be enthusiastic:
  Sure. I like bowling!   Yes, I'd love to.   Cool!
- When you decline, explain why, and say that you're sorry:
  I'd love to, really, but I'm busy.
  Tonight? I'm sorry, I can't. Another day perhaps?
- Use intonation to sound enthusiastic or sorry.

7 A ▶ 3.15 Read the Skill box. Listen to the conversations. Does speaker B accept (✔) or decline (✘) the invitations?

1 **A** Would you like to go out for dinner tonight?   **B** ____
2 **A** Do you want to have a barbecue this weekend?   **B** ____
3 **A** How about going swimming tomorrow?   **B** ____
4 **A** Do you want to have lunch on Saturday?   **B** ____

B ▶ 3.15 Listen again. Repeat speaker B's words. Copy his/her intonation.

Go to Communication practice: Student A page 159, Student B page 168

8 A **PREPARE** Think of an activity you want to do with a friend. Use the places in the boxes or your own ideas.

cinema   bowling alley   café   restaurant   shopping centre   museum   gallery   gym

B **PRACTISE** Invite your partner to do your activity and accept or decline your partner's invitation politely. Agree a time and place if you accept.

C **PERSONAL BEST** In groups of four, repeat your conversations and listen to the other pair. Do they use the phrases from the Conversation builder and Skill box correctly?

Personal Best   How often do you go out in the evening during the week? Describe what you normally do.

UNIT 4 Home and away

LANGUAGE prepositions of time ■ daily routine verbs

4A 24 hours in the dark

1 Do you usually do these things in the morning? Discuss in pairs.

> check emails   go to the gym   have a bath   have a shower   have breakfast

Go to Vocabulary practice: daily routine verbs, page 142

2 A Look at the title of the lesson and the pictures in the text. Which countries sometimes have 24 hours of darkness?

B Read the text. Match the headings in the box with the paragraphs A–E.

> Light and dark   Summer activities   Our daily routine   My city   Winter activities

24 hours of night – or day!
by Tom Sanders

A _____
I'm from New York, but I now live in the north of Norway in a small city called Tromsø. I like living here. I have an interesting job and I like the people.

B _____
I work from 8.00 in the morning to 4.00 in the afternoon. I usually wake up at 6.00 and get up at 6.15. I have a shower and get dressed. At 6.45, I have breakfast and check my emails. I leave home at 7.15. My wife and children leave home at 8.00. The children start school at 8.30 and finish at 2.30. I get home at about 5.00.

C _____
Our lives are different in the summer and the winter. In the summer, there are 60 days when the sun doesn't set. From May to July, it's light at midnight. And in the winter, we have 60 days of night. From November to January, it's dark at midday!

D _____
It's very dark, but it isn't a bad time of year. At the weekend, we spend time together as a family or we go skiing. We sometimes see the Northern Lights at night. They're really beautiful.

E _____
In the summer, we spend a lot of time outdoors. In the evening, we often have a barbecue on the beach and, on Friday nights, we sometimes go to outdoor concerts. In July, we go on holiday. We usually visit my family in New York and also spend some time with my wife's family in the mountains.

30

prepositions of time ■ daily routine verbs **LANGUAGE** **4A**

3 A Read paragraph B again. Cover the text. Ask and answer questions about Tom and his family's daily routine with the verb phrases in the box. What can you remember?

wake up   have breakfast   leave home   start work/school   finish work/school   get home

A *When does Tom wake up?*   **B** *I think he wakes up at 6.00.*

B In pairs, compare your daily routine with Tom's. What is the same? What is different?
I have breakfast at home, too.   I don't check my emails at home.   I get home at six o'clock, not five o'clock.

4 Choose the correct prepositions to complete the sentences. Use the text to help you. Then read the Grammar box.
1 I leave home *at / in* 7.15.
2 *In / From* May *on / to* July, it's light *at / in* midnight.
3 We sometimes see the Northern Lights *in / at* night.
4 *At / In* the summer, we spend a lot of time outdoors.
5 *On / At* Friday nights, we sometimes go to outdoor concerts.

Grammar	prepositions of time		
in:	**on:**	**at:**	**from ... to:**
the morning(s)	Saturday(s)	5.30	... Monday ... Friday
the winter	Friday night(s)	midnight/midday	... November ... January
July	Monday morning(s)	the weekend	... 9.00 a.m. ... 5.00 p.m.

Go to Grammar practice: prepositions of time, page 118

5 A Read about Tom's daughter, Mia. Complete the sentences with the correct prepositions.
1 I usually wake up _____ 5.45 on weekdays.
2 I swim _____ 6.30 _____ 7.30. _____ the weekend, I get up _____ the afternoon!
3 _____ Fridays and Saturdays, I go to bed late.
4 _____ the summer, I often go to concerts _____ night. They don't finish until 2.00 _____ the morning, but it's still light.

B ▶ 4.3 Listen and check your answers. What does Mia love doing? Do you enjoy this activity?

6 ▶ 4.4 **Pronunciation:** sentence stress Listen and repeat the sentences. Which words are stressed?
1 I get up at six in the morning.
2 I work from Monday to Friday.
3 I go swimming on Wednesday evenings.
4 I walk to work in the summer.
5 My wife gets home at midnight.
6 We have dinner at 8.30.

7 A Complete the sentences so that they are true for you. Write one false sentence.
1 I get up at _____.
2 I work from _____.
3 I _____ evenings.
4 I _____ the summer.
5 I don't _____ the weekend.

B In pairs, say your sentences. Guess the false sentences.

Go to Communication practice: Student A page 160, Student B page 169

8 A Read and answer the questions. Are you a morning person or an evening person?
1 What time do you usually get up at the weekend?
2 What time do you usually go to bed at the weekend?
3 When do you like working or studying?
4 When do you enjoy doing exercise?

B Find a classmate who is like you. Discuss what you like doing in the morning or in the evening. Tell the rest of your class.
David and I are morning people. We like getting up early and going to the gym before work.

Personal Best Think of someone that you know well. Describe his/her daily routine during the week and at the weekend.

31

4 SKILLS

LISTENING listening for the main idea ■ sentence stress ■ the weather and the seasons

4B Weather around the world

1 Complete the sentences with the words in the box.

snowing   hot   cold   raining   cloudy   foggy

1 It's _____.   2 It's _____.   3 It's _____.   4 It's _____.   5 It's _____.   6 It's _____.

Go to Vocabulary practice: the weather and the seasons, page 142

2 A Complete the table. Then tell your partner about the activities that you do in different seasons.

Season	Months	Weather	My activities

B What is your favourite season? Why? Tell your partner.

> **Skill   listening for the main idea(s)**
>
> It is important to understand the main idea when someone is speaking.
> - Use any pictures to help you understand what the topic is.
> - Think about who is speaking and what the situation is.
> - Don't worry if you don't understand everything. Listen for the important words.

3 ▶ 4.6 Read the Skill box. Watch or listen to the first part of *Learning Curve*. Match places 1–4 with the types of weather a–d.

1 New York   a rainy and very cloudy
2 Mount Emei   b usually warm
3 Bay of Bengal   c very rainy
4 Rome   d sometimes snowy in winter

4 ▶ 4.6 Watch or listen again. For 1–3, tick (✓) the correct sentence, a or b.

1
a ☐ It never snows in autumn in New York.
b ☐ Ethan wears his snow boots every day in winter.
2
a ☐ It rains a lot in Mount Emei, but it rains more in the Bay of Bengal.
b ☐ It's very cloudy in the Bay of Bengal.
3
a ☐ It doesn't often snow in Rome.
b ☐ When it snows in New York, the schools always close.

listening for the main idea ■ sentence stress ■ the weather and the seasons   LISTENING   SKILLS 4B

5 ▶ 4.7 Watch or listen to the second part of the show. For each sentence, write M (Marina), S (Sam) or J (Jenny).

Marina

Sam

Jenny

1 Once in 100 years, there's snow! _____
2 I get about 100 days of sun a year. _____
3 It's like this 200 days a year. _____
4 I love it. Winter is here! _____
5 I sleep early and wake up early. _____
6 We don't usually talk about the weather. _____

6 ▶ 4.7 Watch or listen again. Choose the correct options to complete the sentences.
1 Marina says it's *17°C* / *−7°C* / *18°C*.
2 She goes to her sister's house *after breakfast* / *in the afternoon* / *in the evening*.
3 Sam says it's *sometimes* / *usually* / *always* hot and sunny in Egypt.
4 His advice is to *wear a hat* / *wear boots* / *carry an umbrella* in hot weather.
5 Jenny says the weather forecast is good for *Saturday* / *Monday* / *Tuesday*.
6 She *likes* / *doesn't like* / *hates* living in Newfoundland.

7 In pairs, think of some advice for visitors to your country for different seasons.
In the winter, it's a good idea to wear warm clothes.

Listening builder | sentence stress

In English, we usually stress the most important words in a sentence. These stressed words are usually nouns, verbs, adjectives and adverbs. You can usually understand the general idea if you only hear these words:
<u>Mount Emei</u> in <u>China</u> gets <u>twenty-seven feet</u> of <u>rain</u> in a <u>year</u>.
In the <u>evening</u>, we have <u>dinner</u> at my <u>sister's house</u>.

8 A Read the Listening builder. Read the text and <u>underline</u> the most important words.

Patagonia is a beautiful part of South America. It's always windy in Patagonia. The wind is sometimes very strong – about a hundred and twenty kilometres an hour. You can't walk when it's so windy.

B ▶ 4.8 Listen and check which words are stressed.

9 Discuss the questions in pairs.
1 Do people in your country talk about the weather a lot?
2 Do you talk about the weather a lot? Who do you talk about it with?
3 What kinds of weather do you like? (sunny weather, rainy weather, etc.)
4 What kinds of weather do you hate?
5 What do people do in your country when the weather is bad?
6 Do you sometimes have strange weather? Describe it.

Personal Best Write a guide to the weather in your country for tourists.

33

4 LANGUAGE — present continuous

4C A long weekend

1 What do you like doing when you visit a new city? Tell your partner.

2 A In pairs, look at the pictures of Charlotte and Pete's trip. Which city are they in?

B Read Charlotte's posts. Which famous places does she mention?

3 Read the posts again. Answer the questions.
1. Do they like their apartment?
2. What's the weather like?
3. How do they travel around?
4. Do they like the food?

a
We're going away for a long weekend. I'm so excited! We're sitting on the train and we're waiting to leave for Paris on the Eurostar. I'm having a good time already!

b
We're here. We're staying in a private apartment with a view of the city. It's so romantic!

c
Today, we're visiting the Rodin Museum. We're walking around the beautiful gardens in the warm spring sunshine.

d
Look, it's the Eiffel Tower! I feel like a real tourist. We're having a sandwich and waiting in the queue.

e
I'm having a good time, but Pete isn't happy. We're going shopping on the Champs-Élysées. He's carrying my bags. I'm feeling hungry – time for lunch.

f
We're at a lovely little restaurant. I'm having the steak! The weather's lovely and warm. What's Pete doing? He's trying to speak French to the waiter.

g
It's late. We're tired and we're getting a taxi back to the apartment after a great night out. The city lights are amazing!

h
It's our last day. We're buying some food to take home. It's raining, but we don't mind.

4 Match Pete's posts 1–8 with pictures a–h.
1. I'm looking for some French cheese as a present for my mum.
2. The weather's great. We're having a fun time at the museum.
3. We're going to Paris!
4. What a cool apartment! Charlotte's having a shower and I'm relaxing after the journey.
5. We're visiting a very famous monument. I want to take a selfie at the top.
6. I'm not enjoying this! I hate shopping!
7. We're going back to the apartment now. Brilliant night out!
8. Finally, I'm sitting down! What's for lunch?

5 A <u>Underline</u> the verbs in exercise 4. Which ones describe an action that is happening now?

B Choose *be* or *have* to complete the rule. Then read the Grammar box.

We form the present continuous with the verb *be* / *have* + *-ing* form.

34

present continuous LANGUAGE **4C**

📖 **Grammar** present continuous

Positive:
I**'m having** a good time.
He**'s carrying** my bags.
We**'re getting** a taxi home.

Negative:
I**'m not enjoying** this.
It **isn't raining**.

Questions and short answers:
What**'s** Pete **doing**?
Are you **eating** steak?
Yes, I **am**.   No, I**'m not**.

Go to Grammar practice: present continuous, page 119

6 A ▶ 4.10 **Pronunciation:** linking consonants and vowels Listen and repeat the sentences.
I'm getting‿up.   It‿isn't raining.   He's‿eating‿a sandwich.

B ▶ 4.11 Listen and underline the words that are linked. Listen, check and repeat.
1 What are you talking about?
2 I'm not enjoying this game.
3 We're sitting in a café.
4 They're going away for a weekend.

7 Complete the dialogues with the present continuous form of the verbs. Then act out the dialogues in pairs.
1 **A** What _____ you _____ (do) here?   **B** I _____ (wait) for my friends.
2 **A** _____ it _____ (snow)?   **B** No, it _____. It _____ (rain).
3 **A** Why _____ James _____ (wear) a suit?   **B** He _____ (go) to a job interview.
4 **A** _____ your friends _____ (leave) now?   **B** Yes, they _____. They _____ (look) for their umbrellas.
5 **A** Who _____ Ben _____ (phone)?   **B** I don't know. He _____ (not / talk) to Ryan because Ryan's here!

Go to Communication practice: Student A page 160, Student B page 169

8 Work in groups. Take turns to mime and guess the actions.

A *Are you getting dressed?*   **B** *No, I'm not.*   **A** *Are you having a shower?*   **B** *Yes, I am!*

9 A Charlotte phones her friend, Olivia. Complete the conversation with the correct form of the verbs in the box. Who is Nacho?

visit   have   do   make   play   wait

Olivia Hello, Charlotte! How are you?
Charlotte Hi, Olivia! I'm good, thanks. I'm in Paris with Pete! We ¹_____ a great time!
Olivia Paris! That's fantastic. What ²_____ at the moment?
Charlotte We're at the Eiffel Tower. We ³_____ to go up. Where are you?
Olivia I ⁴_____ my parents-in-law with Nacho and the girls. They ⁵_____ in the garden with Nacho's mum. And Nacho's dad ⁶_____ lunch for us.
Charlotte That sounds nice.

B ▶ 4.12 Listen and check your answers.

10 Imagine you are on holiday. Decide where you are. Phone your partner and tell each other where you are, who you are with and what you are doing.
A *Hello, Ana. It's Daniel.*   **B** *Hi! Where are you?*   **A** *I'm in London. I'm going for a walk in Hyde Park.*

Personal Best Imagine your long weekend. Write eight sentences to describe what you're doing.

4 SKILLS   WRITING   describing a photo ■ using personal pronouns

4D A holiday with friends

1 Ask and answer the questions in pairs.

1 When do you go on holiday?
2 Where do you usually go?
3 Who do you go with?
4 What do you like doing there?

2 **A** Look at the pictures. Guess where the people are.
   B Read the email and check.

Hi Lucy,

¹ How are you? How's work? I hope everything's OK.

² I'm in Argentina! I'm visiting Leo and Maria in Buenos Aires, and I'm having a wonderful time. The weather's amazing! It's 25 degrees and it's never cloudy. It's hot all day and warm at night. It's so nice after the cold autumn weather at home.

³ Most days I get up early here and I go for a run with Leo before breakfast. He loves doing sport in the morning. Then we return home and have breakfast. Leo and Maria start work at 8.30, and I leave the apartment with them. I go into the city and visit different places like Casa Rosada and Teatro Colón. In the evening, we go for a walk and then have dinner. The restaurants are great here and the steaks are fantastic!

⁴ I'm sending you a couple of photos that I took. The first photo's of some colourful houses in an area called La Boca. It's a really cool part of town with some amazing buildings. In the second photo, you can see Leo and Maria. We're having a coffee at a local café near their apartment. It sells great coffee and delicious pastries.

My flight's on Friday. See you at work on Monday!

Love, Gemma

---

3 Read the email again. In which paragraph does Gemma …

1 write about the weather? _____
2 describe the pictures? _____
3 ask Lucy questions? _____
4 write about her daily routine on holiday? _____

> **Skill** describing a photo
>
> When you send a photo, describe who or what the photo shows. If it shows people, describe what they are doing:
> The first photo's of some colourful houses. In the second photo, you can see …
> In this photo, I'm in the park with my friends. We're playing football.
> This photo's of my sister. She's playing the piano. Here's a photo of our new car.

4 Read the Skill box. Look at Gemma's email again. How does she describe the pictures?

describing a photo ■ using personal pronouns   WRITING   SKILLS   4D

5 A Match the halves to make complete sentences.

1 In this photo, I'm with
2 Here's a photo
3 In this photo, we're
4 Here's a photo of us in

a Red Square in Moscow!
b repairing our bikes.
c of Sydney at night.
d my niece, Eliza. We're reading a story.

B Match the completed sentences with pictures a–d.

Text builder   using personal pronouns

We often use personal pronouns (*he*, *she*, *it*, etc.) to avoid repeating words and names:
*I'm with Sergio and Ana. **We**'re eating fish. **It**'s delicious!*
*Eleni's helping me with my French homework. **She** speaks really good French.*

6 A Read the Text builder. Read paragraphs 3 and 4 in the email again and underline the personal pronouns. What do they refer to?

B Complete the sentences with the correct personal pronouns.

1 I'm with Theo. _____'re waiting for the train.
2 This is the hotel pool. _____'s on top of the hotel.
3 Theo's shopping. _____'s spending all his money!
4 Katie's in bed. _____'s sleeping!
5 The kids are out. _____'re on their bikes.

7 A PREPARE   Imagine you're on holiday. Decide where you are, what the weather's like, how you're feeling, who is with you and what you do every day. Imagine two or three photos of your holiday.

B PRACTISE   Write an email to a friend. Use personal pronouns to avoid repeating words/names.

• Begin your email.
• Paragraph 1: Ask your friend how he/she is.
• Paragraph 2: Describe where you are, what the weather is like and who is with you.
• Paragraph 3: Describe your daily routine on holiday.
• Paragraph 4: Describe two or three photos of your holiday.
• Finish your email.

C PERSONAL BEST   Swap emails with a partner. Does his/her email contain personal pronouns to avoid repeating words/names? Can you add any more?

Personal Best   Find a photo of people on holiday. Describe their holiday. Where are they? What are they doing?

3 and 4 REVIEW and PRACTICE

Grammar

1 Choose the correct options to complete the sentences.

1 This week _____ in Cambridge.
   a I stay
   b I staying
   c I'm staying

2 What _____ at the moment?
   a do you do
   b are you doing
   c doing you

3 My grandfather always _____ on Sunday afternoons.
   a is visiting
   b visit
   c visits

4 _____ do you see your cousins?
   a How many
   b How often
   c How about

5 My sister's birthday is _____ Friday.
   a at
   b in
   c on

6 My brother's in his room with a friend. _____ computer games.
   a They playing
   b They're playing
   c They play

7 I _____ at the weekend.
   a play always football
   b always play football
   c play football always

8 When _____ go shopping?
   a do you usually
   b usually do you
   c are you

2 Complete the dialogue with the correct form of the verb in brackets.

A How [1]_____ (be) the new job?
B It's good. At the moment, I [2]_____ (work) on a new project.
A Where?
B Near Edinburgh. We [3]_____ (build) a new hotel.
A Where [4]_____ (live) at the moment?
B I'm living with friends from Monday to Friday and then I always [5]_____ (come) home at the weekend.
A Are you OK with that?
B I don't mind [6]_____ (travel) and I enjoy [7]_____ (work) in a small team.
A No problems at all?
B Well, I hate [8]_____ (get up) early on Monday mornings!

3 Complete the text with the words in the box.

flies   at   often   arrives   stays
checks   starts   spends

I live in six cities

Barbara Fiala is the owner of Baobab, a communications company, based in New York. She [1]_____ travels for work and spends around two months a year in Europe. She [2]_____ to London and then visits Berlin, Budapest and Warsaw. She usually [3]_____ three nights in each city and then starts again. She [4]_____ in the evening, so she's ready to work the next day. 'I often go for a walk or go to the gym [5]_____ 6 a.m,' she says. She [6]_____ work around 7 a.m. and [7]_____ her emails and makes some telephone calls before her meetings. In London, she [8]_____ with her sister, but in the other cities she goes to hotels. She does yoga and reads books to relax.

Vocabulary

1 Circle the word that is different. Explain your answer.

1 son	father	niece	brother
2 autumn	rain	spring	winter
3 yoga	barbecue	picnic	takeaway
4 golf	bowling	volleyball	dancing
5 cold	snowy	warm	icy
6 gallery	museum	gym	violin
7 aunt	grandmother	son	mother
8 karate	swimming	shopping	cycling

REVIEW and PRACTICE 3 and 4

2 Make words to describe the weather.

What's the weather like? It's _____ .

1 d y o c u l _____
2 n d w y i _____
3 t h o _____
4 g y o g f _____
5 m r w a _____
6 y u n s n _____
7 i a n r y _____
8 w o n s y _____

3 Put the words in the correct columns.

summer	school	son	swimming	gym	spring
shopping	sister	home	winter	cycling
uncle	autumn	cousin	yoga	museum

Seasons	Relatives	Activities	Places

4 Complete the sentences with the correct form of the verbs in the box.

| do | leave | start | walk | get | play | go | have |

1 My father _____ up in the morning at six o'clock.
2 He works in a factory and _____ work at 7.30 a.m.
3 I usually _____ to work at 10.00 a.m. on Fridays.
4 To keep fit I _____ karate at lunchtime.
5 I _____ work at five in the evening and cycle home.
6 In the evening, I _____ my dog for an hour.
7 My sister _____ the violin.
8 We often _____ dinner together.

Personal Best

Lesson 3A — Name five relatives.

Lesson 4A — Write three things you do every evening.

Lesson 3A — Write two sentences using adverbs of frequency.

Lesson 4A — Think of three time expressions beginning 'In…'.

Lesson 3B — Write a sentence using *also*.

Lesson 4C — List three things you can do during a weekend in another city.

Lesson 3C — Describe two things you like doing, one in the week and one at weekends.

Lesson 4C — Write a question and answer using the present continuous.

Lesson 3D — Write three times of the day which are important to you.

Lesson 4C — Write a negative sentence using the present continuous.

Lesson 3D — Give two expressions used for agreeing a time to meet a friend.

Lesson 4D — Describe where you are, what you're doing and the weather.

UNIT 5

What are you wearing?

LANGUAGE present simple and present continuous ▪ clothes ▪ ordinal numbers

5A Party time

1 Look at the pictures in the text. What are the people wearing? Choose from the words in the box.

a dress   a shirt   trousers   boots   a jacket   sandals   a hat   a suit

Go to Vocabulary practice: clothes, page 143

2 **A** Read the text. Match pictures a–c with the names of the celebrations 1–3.

B Match sentences 1–5 with the three celebrations.

1 This celebration takes place in Brazil.   _____
2 A lot of people wear red for this celebration. _____
3 This celebration starts on a Friday.   _____
4 This celebration happens in the winter.   _____
5 Animals take part in this celebration.   _____

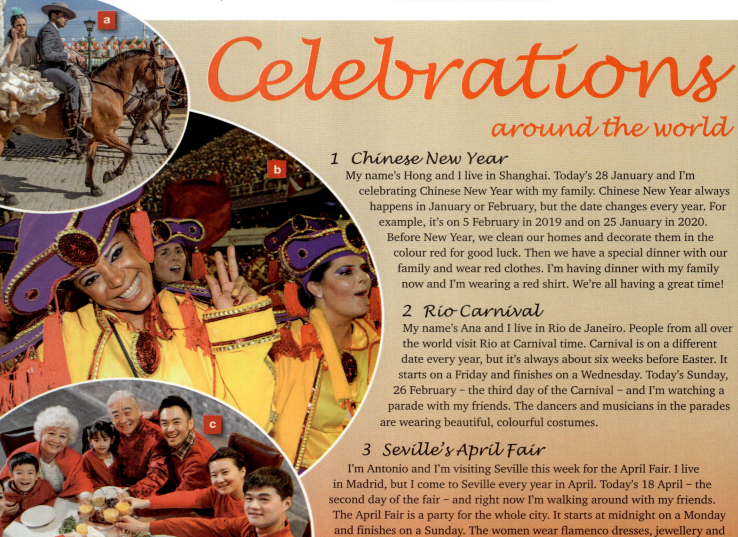

Celebrations
around the world

1 Chinese New Year

My name's Hong and I live in Shanghai. Today's 28 January and I'm celebrating Chinese New Year with my family. Chinese New Year always happens in January or February, but the date changes every year. For example, it's on 5 February in 2019 and on 25 January in 2020. Before New Year, we clean our homes and decorate them in the colour red for good luck. Then we have a special dinner with our family and wear red clothes. I'm having dinner with my family now and I'm wearing a red shirt. We're all having a great time!

2 Rio Carnival

My name's Ana and I live in Rio de Janeiro. People from all over the world visit Rio at Carnival time. Carnival is on a different date every year, but it's always about six weeks before Easter. It starts on a Friday and finishes on a Wednesday. Today's Sunday, 26 February – the third day of the Carnival – and I'm watching a parade with my friends. The dancers and musicians in the parades are wearing beautiful, colourful costumes.

3 Seville's April Fair

I'm Antonio and I'm visiting Seville this week for the April Fair. I live in Madrid, but I come to Seville every year in April. Today's 18 April – the second day of the fair – and right now I'm walking around with my friends. The April Fair is a party for the whole city. It starts at midnight on a Monday and finishes on a Sunday. The women wear flamenco dresses, jewellery and flowers in their hair, and the men wear suits and hats. Some people ride horses. The atmosphere's brilliant!

present simple and present continuous ■ clothes ■ ordinal numbers   LANGUAGE 5A

3 A <u>Underline</u> the verbs in the present simple and (circle) the verbs in the present continuous in the text.

B Complete the rules with *simple* or *continuous*. Then read the Grammar box.
1 We use the present _____ to talk about facts and things that happen regularly.
2 We use the present _____ to talk about things that are happening now or temporary actions.

Grammar present simple and present continuous

For things that happen regularly or are always true, we use the present simple:
It always **happens** in January or February.   I **live** in Shanghai.

For things that are happening now or temporary actions, we use the present continuous:
I'**m having** dinner with my family now.   I'**m visiting** Seville this week.

Go to Grammar practice: present simple and present continuous, page 120

4 A Complete the interview with the correct form of the verbs in brackets. Which person from the text is the interview with?

A Hello. I'm from 103 FM Radio. ¹_____ you _____ a good time? (have)
B Yes, it's amazing! We ²_____ every year. (come)
A What ³_____ you _____ at the moment? (do)
B We ⁴_____ the local people go past on their horses. (watch) The women look beautiful!
A What ⁵_____ they _____? (wear)
B Long flamenco dresses with special sandals, lots of jewellery and flowers in their hair. People at the fair always ⁶_____ traditional clothes like that. (wear)
A ⁷_____ you _____ here? (live)
B No, I ⁸_____ just _____ the city this week. (visit) It's my favourite festival in the whole country.
A Great to talk to you! Enjoy the rest of the celebration.

B ▶5.3 Listen and check your answers.

Go to Communication practice: Student A page 161, Student B page 170

5 Match festivals 1–5 with the dates a–e.
1 Christmas Day   a 8 March
2 New Year's Day   b 31 October
3 Halloween   c 1 January
4 Valentine's Day   d 25 December
5 International Women's Day   e 14 February

Go to Vocabulary practice: ordinal numbers, page 143

6 A ▶5.5 **Pronunciation:** dates Listen and repeat the dates. Which words are stressed?

It's the second of May.   It's the third of June.   It's July the fourteenth.   It's August the twenty-fifth.

B ▶5.6 In pairs, say each date in two different ways. Listen, check and repeat.

It's the first of April.   It's April the first.

1 1 April   5 31 October   9 February 26
2 4 July   6 November 20   10 March 5
3 8 August   7 December 30
4 12 September   8 January 16

7 A Ask different classmates about their birthdays. Who has a birthday in the same month as you?
A *When's your birthday?* B *My birthday's on the seventh of March.*
A *What do you usually do on your birthday?* B *I usually go out for lunch with my family. What about you?*

B Tell the class about your classmates' birthdays.

Elena's birthday's on the fourth of June. She always goes out with her friends.

Personal Best Write sentences about some of your classmates. What do they usually wear to class? What are they wearing today?

41

5 SKILLS READING identifying facts and opinions ■ adjectives

5B Don't tell me what to wear

1 Read the introduction of the text and discuss the questions in pairs.

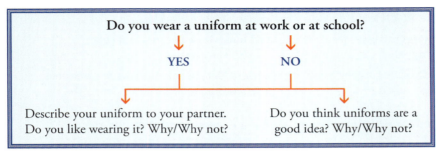

Skill   identifying facts and opinions

Texts often include both facts and opinions.
A fact is a piece of true information: *New Year's Day is on 1 January*.
An opinion is what someone thinks about something. You can express an opinion with:
a verb: *I think (that) …, I don't think (that) …, I agree, I don't agree*
a positive or negative adjective: *good, fun, lovely, bad, horrible*

2 **A** Read the Skill box and the text. Find one fact for each person.
1 Richard _____   4 Nikki _____
2 Maria _____   5 Hannah _____
3 Saif _____

B In pairs, say your facts. Do you remember which person says them?
A *I wear a uniform in my job – a hat, a shirt and trousers.* **B** *That's Hannah.*

3 Read the text again and answer the questions.
Which person/people think(s) that …
1 uniforms aren't for everyone? _____
2 his/her uniform isn't nice? _____
3 his/her uniform is nice? _____, _____
4 his/her uniform isn't interesting? _____
5 uniforms are a good idea in his/her situation? _____, _____, _____, _____

Text builder   adjectives

Adjectives often show someone's opinion:
*It's quite **boring**.*   *We have a **nice** uniform at the bank.*   *The hat's **terrible**.*

Adjectives come before a noun and after the verb *be*:
*We wear a **brilliant** uniform.*   *The uniform's **brilliant**!*

4 Read the Text builder. Find more examples of adjectives in the text. Does each one come before a noun or after the verb *be*?

5 Look at the pictures. Imagine you wear one of the uniforms. Write a paragraph about your uniform. Give facts and opinions.

42

identifying facts and opinions ■ adjectives   READING   SKILLS   5B

UNIFORMS
ARE YOU A FAN?

Uniforms are common for schoolchildren, police officers, firefighters, soldiers and a lot of other jobs. But do people like wearing uniforms? Does a uniform make you feel part of a group or do people dislike looking exactly the same? Here, five readers give us their opinions.

Richard, 16
I wear a uniform to school every day. The uniform for boys is black shoes or trainers, black trousers, a white shirt and a blue jumper. It's quite boring, but I don't mind wearing it. I think it's OK to have a school uniform. It means my parents don't need to buy lots of clothes.

Maria, 27
I work in fashion and clothes are a big part of my life. I always wear stylish suits to work. It's important to look good in my job – your clothes say a lot about you. Uniforms are fine for some people, but not for me. I don't want someone telling me what to wear.

Saif, 40
Everyone knows we wear a uniform in the fire service. We wear special boots, trousers, jackets, gloves and helmets because we need them. It also shows people that we're firefighters – we're there to help them. I think our uniform's brilliant! It makes me feel part of the fire service.

Nikki, 35
We have a nice uniform in my bank – the women all wear a smart jacket, a white shirt and scarf, and trousers or a skirt. It makes life simple because you don't need to choose your clothes in the morning! I think the uniform's quite fashionable, too – it's similar to my own clothes.

Hannah, 21
I wear a uniform in my job – a hat, a shirt and trousers. I don't like my uniform. I don't like the material and the hat's terrible. But I agree that uniforms are necessary in my job because they often get dirty and I don't want to wear my own clothes at work.

Personal Best — Choose a profession and design an ideal uniform for men and for women. Write a description of it.

5 LANGUAGE *can* and *can't* ■ hobbies

5C Do the things you love

1 Work in pairs. Match the verbs in the box with the pictures 1–5 in the text.

> sew   bake   take photos   paint   make jewellery

Go to Vocabulary practice: hobbies, page 144

2 **A** Read the webpage. Which people don't have another job?

B Read the webpage again and answer the questions.
1 How does Sandra make money?
2 What does Paul paint?
3 Do people buy Alexa's photos directly from her?
4 Where does Edith sell her clothes?
5 Where do people buy Alain's cakes?

MONEY MONTHLY
Do the things you love

Do you have a hobby? Perhaps you write a blog, collect stamps or play chess. Or maybe you draw or paint. These are all great hobbies and many people enjoy doing them for pleasure, but can you make money from your hobby? Read this week's article and find out.

Meet Sandra, Paul, Alexa, Edith and Alain. They all make money from their hobbies.

SANDRA works full time in an office, but in her free time, she makes jewellery. She started making jewellery when she was a girl and now makes earrings, bracelets and rings, and sells them online. She can earn about £100 a month from her hobby. She also wears some of the things she makes.

PAUL's a teacher and, in his free time, he paints. He paints beautiful paintings of animals. People often ask him to paint their pets. He usually goes to their homes to see the pets, draws a picture and then finishes the painting in his studio at home. He sells about ten paintings every year.

ALEXA's a nurse and her hobby is photography. She has three different cameras. She usually visits interesting places at the weekends. She takes great photos and she often uploads her photos to photo libraries. People can't use them for free, but they can pay to download them.

EDITH AND ALAIN are retired. Edith can sew and make dresses, shirts and trousers. She sells her clothes at the local market. Alain loves cooking and he bakes delicious cakes. He sells them to local cafés and people love them. 'It's great,' he says. 'I can make money simply by doing what I love!'

---

3 Complete the sentences from the text with the phrases in the box.

> can't use   can pay   can make   can earn

1 She _____ about £100 a month.
2 People _____ them for free.
3 They _____ to download them.
4 I _____ money simply by doing what I love.

can and *can't* ■ hobbies   LANGUAGE **5C**

4 Look at the sentences in exercise 3. Choose the correct options to complete the rules. Then read the Grammar box.
1 We put an infinitive *with* / *without* 'to' after *can*.
2 The *he* and *she* form of *can* is *the same as* / *different from* the other forms.
3 The negative form of *can* is *can't* / *don't can*.

> **Grammar** *can* and *can't*
>
> *can* to talk about ability:
> He **can** make money by doing what he loves.
> She **can** sew.
>
> *can* to talk about possibility:
> People **can** pay to download them.
> You **can** buy Alain's cakes in this shop.
>
> *can* to talk about permission:
> You **can** park here.   We **can** sit here.
>
> Negative:
> People **can't** use them for free.
>
> Questions and short answers:
> **Can** you make money from your hobby?
> Yes, I **can**.   No, I **can't**.

Go to Grammar practice: *can* and *can't*, page 121

5 A ▶ 5.9 **Pronunciation:** *can* and *can't* Listen and repeat.
1 My brother can speak Italian.
2 I can ride a bike.
3 My sister can't play the violin.
4 You can't sit there.
5 **A** Can you knit? **B** Yes, I can.
6 **A** Can John play chess? **B** No, he can't.

B ▶ 5.10 Say the sentences. Listen, check and repeat.
1 I can't swim.
2 You can sell your cakes here.
3 **A** Can I ask you a question? **B** Yes, you can.
4 David can't sew.
5 Ellie can sing.
6 **A** Can you cook French food? **B** No, I can't.

Go to Communication practice: Student A page 161, Student B page 170

6 A Imagine you are the manager of a shop. Decide the rules for your shop assistants. Complete the sentences with *can* or *can't*.

1 You _____ wear your own clothes at work.
2 You _____ read magazines in the shop.
3 You _____ drink tea and coffee when you're at work.
4 You _____ use your phone in the shop.
5 You _____ choose what time you have lunch.
6 You _____ have a discount when you buy things in the shop.

B In pairs, ask and answer questions about your rules. Do you want to work in your partner's shop? Why/Why not?

A *Can I wear my own clothes at work?*   **B** *No, you can't. Everyone wears a uniform.*

7 A Match sentences 1–5 with headings a–e.
1 You can't go swimming in the sea here because we don't have a beach.
2 I can bake really good biscuits.
3 You can drive a car if you're over eighteen.
4 You can visit the Science Museum.
5 I can't speak Japanese.

a Your abilities: things that you can do
b Your abilities: things that you can't do
c Things that people can do in your town or city
d Things that people can't do in your town or city
e Things that you can do in your country if you're over eighteen

B Think of more sentences that are true for you in pairs.
In our city, you can watch a football match at the national stadium.

Personal Best Write about your favourite hobby. When do you do it? Do you do it with other people? Can you earn money from it?   45

5 SKILLS SPEAKING shopping for clothes ■ offering help

5D Can I try it on?

1 A Do you enjoy shopping for these things? Why/Why not? Tell your partner.

books   food   clothes   shoes   jewellery   sports equipment   birthday presents

B Do you like shopping in these places?

department stores   supermarkets   markets   local shops   online   shopping centres

2 ▶ 5.11 Watch or listen to the first part of *Learning Curve*. Are the sentences true (T) or false (F)?
1 Simon, Kate and Jack all want some new clothes. ____
2 They have a big event next week. ____
3 They want to order things online. ____

3 ▶ 5.11 Watch or listen again. Choose the correct options to complete the sentences.
1 Simon *likes / loves / doesn't mind* shopping for sports equipment.
2 He *likes / doesn't like / doesn't mind* shopping for birthday presents.
3 He *likes / doesn't like / doesn't mind* shopping at department stores.
4 The big event is a special *dinner / show / party*.
5 'First in Web TV' is a *prize / video channel / website*.

4 ▶ 5.12 Watch or listen to the second part of the show and tick (✓) the clothes that Simon, Jack and Kate try on.

1 coat ☐   6 scarf ☐
2 top ☐   7 shirt ☐
3 skirt ☐   8 dress ☐
4 tie ☐   9 pyjamas ☐
5 suit ☐   10 shorts ☐

5 ▶ 5.12 Match the halves to make complete sentences. Watch or listen again and check.

1 Do you have it   a sell pyjamas?
2 What colours   b this credit card here?
3 Do you   c in a size 38?
4 Where are the   d are there?
5 How much   e these on, please?
6 Can I pay with   f is it?
7 Can I try   g women's changing rooms, please?

shopping for clothes ■ offering help **SPEAKING**   SKILLS **5D**

Conversation builder — shopping for clothes

Asking for information:
Do you have this (suit)/these (jeans) in (blue/a size 38/a medium)?
What colours are there?
Do you sell (pyjamas)?
Where are the women's changing rooms, please?
How much is it/are they?

Asking for permission:
Can I try this (suit) on, please?
Can I pay with cash/by credit card?

this/that/these/those:

I like this (shirt).

I like these (shirts).

I like that (shirt).

I like those (shirts).

6 Read the Conversation builder. Choose two items in the box. In pairs, take turns to ask and answer questions about them. Ask about the prices, sizes (small, medium or large) and colours.

> dress   shirt   jacket   jeans   pyjamas   shorts

A *Do you have this dress in a small?*   B *No, I'm sorry, we don't. We only have it in a large.*

Skill — offering help

If someone needs something, we can offer to help them:
- Ask if they need help: *Are you alright? Do you need any help?*
- Ask if you can help: *Can I help you?*
- Say what you will do: *Just a moment. I'll check.   I'll show you (where they are). Let me ask my colleague. One moment.*

7 ▶ 5.13   Read the Skill box. Complete the conversation. Listen and check.

A ¹_____?
B Yes, please. I'm looking for jackets.
A ²_____.
B Thank you. Do you have this jacket in a large?
A ³_____. One moment. ... Yes. Here you are.
B Thank you very much.

Go to Communication practice: Student A page 161, Student B page 170

8 A PREPARE In pairs, read the situations. Choose your roles. Think about what you need to say.

	Situation 1	Situation 2
Student A	You are a customer. You want to buy a blue T-shirt in a medium. You can spend $20. Ask to try the T-shirt on. Ask about the changing rooms.	You are a shop assistant in a shoe shop. You have shoes in black, brown and blue, in every size. Offer to help the customer.
Student B	You are a shop assistant in a department store. You have white, blue and black T-shirts, in small and medium. They are $19.99. Offer to help the customer.	You are a customer. You want to buy some brown shoes in a size 43. Ask about the price. If it's OK, ask to try the shoes on.

B PRACTISE Act out your conversations.

C PERSONAL BEST Find a new partner and act out your conversations again. Is your conversation better this time?

Personal Best   Write a conversation between a customer and a shop assistant in a clothes shop or department store.

UNIT 6
Homes and cities

LANGUAGE there is/there are, some/any ■ prepositions of place ■ rooms and furniture

6A A small space

1 Look at these rooms and items of furniture. Which of them do you have in your home? Can you think of more?

> kitchen   bedroom   living room   cooker   wardrobe   armchair   sofa   mirror

Go to Vocabulary practice: rooms and furniture, page 145

2 **A** Look at the title of the text and the pictures. How is the apartment special?
  B Read the text and check.

3 Read the text again and answer the questions.
  1 What is Gary's job?
  2 How does Gary make the different 'rooms'?
  3 Where is his bed?
  4 Where can guests sleep?
  5 According to the text, what free-time activities can Gary do in the apartment?

24-room micro-apartment

HONG KONG is a busy and exciting city with a population of more than seven million. Like most people in Hong Kong, architect Gary Chang lives in a small apartment. But Gary's apartment has a difference – he can move the walls. It's only 32 square metres, but he can create a lot of new 'rooms' inside it.

When you come into the apartment, you see just one room. There's a wall with a TV on it. If you move this, you find a kitchen with a sink and cooker. Next to the kitchen, there's a small wall with a washing machine behind it.

Back in the main room, are there any chairs? No, there aren't any armchairs, but there's a small sofa on a wall. You can lift the sofa, pull down the wall and it becomes a double bed! There are some shelves for books next to the bed and there's a desk under the shelves.

Another wall in the main room has shelves for Gary's 3,000 CDs. If you move this wall, you find a bathroom behind it. Is there space for visitors? Gary can cover the bath to make a bed for guests.

In total, Gary can make 24 different 'rooms', including a dining room, a study and a home cinema. There isn't a balcony, but Gary doesn't mind. He has enough space to have dinner with friends, do yoga and even have a party!

there is/there are, some/any ■ prepositions of place ■ rooms and furniture   **LANGUAGE 6A**

4 A Complete the sentences. Check your answers in the text.
1 There _____ a wall with a TV on it.   3 There _____ a balcony.
2 There _____ some shelves for books.   4 There _____ any armchairs.

B Choose the correct options to complete the rules. Then read the Grammar box.
We can use *some* and *any* with plural nouns. They mean 'more than one'.
1 We use *some* / *any* in positive sentences.
2 We use *some* / *any* in negative sentences and plural questions.

> **Grammar**   *there is/there are, some/any*
>
> **Singular**
> Positive: Negative: Questions:
> *There's* a TV.   *There isn't* a sofa.   *Is there* a washing machine?
> *There's* an armchair.   *There isn't* a balcony.   Yes, *there is*.   No, *there isn't*.
>
> **Plural**
> Positive: Negative: Questions:
> *There are some* cupboards. *There aren't any* stairs.   *Are there any* shelves?
>   Yes, *there are*.   No, *there aren't*.
>
> **Look!** We usually use the contraction *there's* for *there is*. We don't contract *there are*.

Go to Grammar practice: *there is/there are, some/any*, page 122

5 A ▶ 6.4 **Pronunciation:** *there's/there are* Listen to the sentences and notice how *there's* and *there are* are pronounced. Listen again and repeat.
1 There's a balcony.   3 There isn't a sofa.
2 There are two armchairs.   4 There aren't any shelves.

B ▶ 6.5 Say the sentences. Listen, check and repeat.
1 There are five rooms in the apartment.   3 There aren't any chairs in the living room.
2 There's a big table in the kitchen.   4 There isn't a garage.

6 A ▶ 6.6 Listen to the description of an apartment. Complete it with the prepositions in the box. Which room is the speaker describing?

> behind   in front of   opposite   under   next to

> This is my favourite room. There's a window [1]_____ the door. There are some chairs and a table [2]_____ the window. We have two comfortable armchairs – they're [3]_____ the TV and there's a small table between them. There are some shelves [4]_____ the armchairs. We have some books and a clock on the shelves. There's a cupboard [5]_____ the TV.

B Underline two other prepositions of place in the text in exercise 6A. Then read the Grammar box.

> **Grammar**   prepositions of place
>
> We use prepositions of place to say where something or someone is:
> Beth's **in** the garden.   The bathroom's **opposite** the bedroom.   Our photos are **on** the shelves.

Go to Grammar practice: prepositions of place, page 122

Go to Communication practice: Student A page 162, Student B page 171

7 Think of a room in your house. What furniture is there? What other objects and possessions are there? Describe it to your partner and ask him/her to draw a plan of it.

Personal Best Write a paragraph about your classroom. Describe what there is.   49

6 SKILLS LISTENING identifying key points ▪ contractions ▪ common adjectives

6B Amazing homes

1 Match the pictures a–h with the adjectives in the box.

> clean   narrow   light   traditional   heavy   wide   modern   dirty

Go to Vocabulary practice: common adjectives, page 145

2 Think of the homes of your friends and family. Describe them to your partner with the adjectives.

My parents' apartment has a modern kitchen and bathroom. There's an old armchair in the living room.

3 A In pairs, look at the pictures from the programme. What adjectives can you use to describe each house?

a   house in the Czech Republic   b   house in the Philippines

B ▶ 6.9   Watch or listen to the first part of *Learning Curve* and check your answers.

4 ▶ 6.9   Watch or listen again. Which house in exercise 3 do sentences 1–5 describe? Write a or b.

1 This house can move up and down.   ___
2 This house is on an island.   ___
3 This house changes with the weather.   ___
4 This house can get bigger.   ___
5 This house is above the ground because it's dry there. ___

Skill identifying key points

When people speak, listen for the important things they say.
- Don't worry if you don't understand every word.
- People often give an example of the key points using *for example*, *such as* or *e.g.*
- Listen to which words are stressed. People often emphasize the most important ideas.

identifying key points ■ contractions ■ common adjectives   LISTENING   SKILLS   6B

5 ▶ 6.10 Read the Skill box. Then watch or listen to the second part of the show. Complete the key points with the names.

Josh

Charlotte

Danielle

Manu

1 _____'s home is very big and very old.
2 _____'s home is small, and it isn't expensive.
3 _____'s only living in this home for a short time.
4 _____'s home has both modern and traditional things.

6 ▶ 6.10 Watch or listen again. Are the sentences true (T) or false (F)?
1 There aren't any windows in Josh's apartment. ____
2 It's quiet in his apartment at night. ____
3 Charlotte has some new things in her kitchen. ____
4 Her wardrobe's very expensive. ____
5 Danielle's house is in Canada. ____
6 She's cleaning the shelves at the moment. ____
7 Manu lives in his beach house for nine months every year. ____
8 He's a teacher in California. ____

7 Discuss the questions in pairs.
1 Do you live in a house or an apartment? How old is it?
2 Are there old or new things in it?
3 Describe your favourite room.
4 Do you live in your house or apartment all year?

Listening builder | contractions

When people speak, they usually contract verbs:
He is calling from California! → He**'s** calling from California!
My home is not big. → My home **isn't** big.
I do not understand. → I **don't** understand.

8 A Read the Listening builder. In pairs, complete the sentences from the programme with the contractions in the box.

don't   there's   it's   I'm   bed's   they're

1 When _____ cold, the house turns and moves up, and gets a lot of sun.
2 I _____ mean a garage at a house.
3 There are about 300 small apartments. And _____ very cheap.
4 My _____ opposite the kitchen.
5 There are four bedrooms and _____ a bathroom next to each bedroom.
6 _____ a teacher!

B ▶ 6.11 Listen and check.

9 Discuss the questions in pairs.
1 What do you remember about the homes in the video?
2 Which homes in the video do you like? Why?
3 Which homes don't you like? Why?
4 Do you prefer modern or traditional homes? Why?
5 Do you know someone who lives in an unusual home? Can you describe it?

Personal Best Write a paragraph about your home or another person's home.

6 LANGUAGE — modifiers ■ places in a city

6C The Big Apple

1 A Think of a city from these continents and regions. Write a fact about each city.

> Europe   Asia   Africa   Latin America   Australasia

B In pairs, tell each other about your cities. Are any of your facts the same?

2 A Look at the pictures. What do you already know about New York City? Make a list in pairs.

B Read the text. What information about New York City is new to you?

So you want to visit … New York City?

New York — 'the Big Apple' — is my favourite city in the world. I love the streets, the modern skyscrapers and old apartment blocks. It's full of really famous sights and even on a short visit you can see a lot of amazing things.

For many people, number one on the list of places to see is the Empire State Building. It's a very famous skyscraper and there are great views of the city from its 86th and 102nd floors. Another interesting skyscraper is 4 Times Square.

It isn't beautiful at all, in my opinion, but it's an important 'green' building. New York has very cold winters and quite hot summers, but 4 Times Square produces its own comfortable temperature for most of the year.

For a fantastic view of Manhattan and the Statue of Liberty, visit Brooklyn Bridge. It's great for taking photos, but it's really busy, with hundreds of cars, bikes and people. If you get stressed out by the noise, go back to Manhattan and relax in City Hall Park for a while. It's quite a small park and it's really pretty. You can have your lunch there and decide what to do next: see a show on Broadway, go shopping on Fifth Avenue or go for a walk in Central Park. It's impossible to be bored in this incredible city!

by Harry Fuller

3 Read the text again. What adjectives does the writer use to describe the places?
1 Empire State Building
2 4 Times Square
3 Brooklyn Bridge
4 City Hall Park

4 Match sentences 1–5 with the pictures a–d. Two sentences match one picture. Then read the Grammar box.
1 This restaurant is very busy.
2 This restaurant isn't very busy.
3 This restaurant is quite busy.
4 This restaurant is really busy.
5 This restaurant isn't busy at all.

a

b

c

d

modifiers ■ places in a city **LANGUAGE 6C**

Grammar: modifiers

We use modifiers with adjectives:
There are **really** beautiful views of the city.
It's **quite** hot in the summer.
It isn't a **very** big park.
It is**n't** a beautiful building **at all**.

Look! When we use *quite* with an adjective + a singular noun, we put it before *a/an*:
It's **quite a** famous building.

Go to Grammar practice: modifiers, page 123

5 Look at the sentences in exercise 4. Rewrite them beginning with *This is*.
This restaurant is very busy. → This is a very busy restaurant.

6 John is staying in a hotel in New York City. Look at his feedback form about the hotel and complete the sentences with *is/isn't* and *very/really* (✓✓), *quite* (✓), *not very* (X) or *(not) … at all* (X X).

In your opinion, this hotel is …					
comfortable	✓	modern	X	nice	✓
clean	✓✓	expensive	✓✓	quiet	X X

John thinks that the hotel …
1 _____ comfortable.   3 _____ modern.   5 _____ nice.
2 _____ clean.   4 _____ expensive.   6 _____ quiet _____.

7 A ▶ 6.13 **Pronunciation:** sentence stress Listen and underline the stressed words in the sentences. Listen, check and repeat.
1 This is a really interesting city.
2 The bridge is quite wide.
3 Our office isn't very nice.
4 The café isn't cheap at all.
5 Their new house is very traditional.
6 It's quite a famous monument.

B ▶ 6.14 Say the sentences. Listen, check and repeat.
1 This apartment is really modern.
2 Pizza Palace isn't a very expensive restaurant.
3 Bristol is quite a nice city.
4 This square is very popular.
5 We live in a really old house.
6 This building isn't beautiful at all.

Go to Communication practice: Student A page 162, Student B page 171

8 Complete definitions 1–3 with the words in the box.

square   churches   apartment blocks   skyscrapers   mosques   market

1 Religious buildings like _____ and _____ are often very beautiful.
2 _____ are very tall buildings. They can be hotels, office blocks and _____.
3 A _____ is an open area in a town or city. There's often a _____ there where you can go shopping.

Go to Vocabulary practice: places in a city, page 146

9 A ▶ 6.16 Listen and match the places with the cities.

mosque
square
stadium
market
theatre
cathedral
skyscraper

Cairo

Brasília

B ▶ 6.16 Listen again and make notes about the places in Cairo and Brasília. Talk about what you can remember in pairs.
You can buy clothes and jewellery at the market in Cairo.

Choose three or four interesting buildings in your city. Write a description of them for a travel website.   53

6 SKILLS WRITING topic sentences ■ describing places

6D Beautiful places

1 A In pairs, match capital cities 1–8 with countries a–h.

1	Kathmandu	a	Kenya
2	Wellington	b	Poland
3	Lima	c	Nepal
4	Warsaw	d	Bulgaria
5	Havana	e	Cuba
6	Nairobi	f	New Zealand
7	Kingston	g	Peru
8	Sofia	h	Jamaica

B Think of ten more capital cities.

2 Read the description of Lisbon. Match pictures a–e with paragraphs 1–5.

a _____

b _____

c _____

d _____

e _____

Lisbon a city by the sea

1 Lisbon's the capital city of Portugal. It's on the River Tejo and it's next to the sea. Lisbon's quite a small capital city – about 550,000 people live there.

2 Lisbon has some very old areas. Alfama and Graça are beautiful old districts with narrow streets, small squares and interesting shops. Above them is the castle of São Jorge. There are wonderful views of the city from the castle. You can walk to Alfama and Graça or you can take the tram. It's a great way to see this part of the city.

3 If you want to go on a day trip, take the tram to Belém. It's the last district before the beach. There are some interesting museums, a cultural centre and some really lovely parks. You can try Belém's famous *pastel de nata*, too. These are delicious custard pastries – perfect with a coffee.

4 There are lots of places to eat, drink and go out in Lisbon. Bairro Alto's a good place for restaurants, music and shops. There are also lots of bars and cafés with musicians and it can be quite noisy at night. If you want a traditional Portuguese restaurant, go to Alfama or Graça.

5 You can visit Lisbon during any season. It isn't very cold in the winter. Spring and autumn are lovely times to visit because it's usually warm and sunny. Summer in Lisbon's very hot, but you can go swimming in the sea to cool down!

3 Write the paragraph number for each topic.

1 old parts of Lisbon ____
2 when to visit ____
3 geographical information ____
4 an interesting day trip ____
5 where to eat and drink ____

topic sentences ■ describing places **WRITING** **SKILLS** **6D**

Skill topic sentences

When you write a text, give each paragraph one main topic. The first sentence of the paragraph introduces the topic – we call it a 'topic sentence'.
For example, in paragraph 1, the 'topic sentence' is: *Lisbon's the capital city of Portugal*.

4 A Read the Skill box. <u>Underline</u> the topic sentences in paragraphs 2–5 of the description of Lisbon.

B In pairs, write a topic sentence for each paragraph about Madrid.

> 1 _____. It's in the middle of the country and it's on the River Manzanares. Madrid's also the political, economic and cultural centre of Spain.
>
> 2 _____. A really old park is El Capricho. This park has a river, a lake and some interesting statues and fountains. Another famous park is El Retiro. This is very popular with families.
>
> 3 _____. You can go to Plaza de Santa Ana, where there are a lot of fantastic bars and restaurants. Other great areas for going out are La Latina, Malasaña and Chueca.

Text builder describing places

Describing a place's location and geography:
... is the capital city of ...
... is in the middle of the country/on the River ... /next to the sea.
... people live there.

Recommending places:
There are wonderful views of ... from ...
If you want to go on a day trip, go to ...
... is a good place for ...
... is a great way to ...
There are lots of places to ...

5 Read the Text builder. Complete the sentences about the city of Santiago.

1 Santiago _____ Chile. _____ River Mapocho.
2 _____, go to Pomaire.
3 _____ the city and the mountains from San Cristóbal Hill.
4 Cycling _____ get to the top of the hill.
5 _____ go out in the evening. Barrio Bellavista _____ restaurants.

6 A **PREPARE** Choose a town or city that you know well. Make notes about the following:

- the location and population
- interesting areas to visit
- places with good views
- places nearby to go on a day trip
- good areas to go out (restaurants, shops, bars, etc.)
- the weather in different seasons

B **PRACTISE** Write a description of your town or city. Begin each paragraph with a topic sentence.

- Paragraph 1: Give geographical information about the location and population.
- Paragraph 2: Describe an interesting area in the city to visit.
- Paragraph 3: Describe a place near the city where people can go on a day trip.
- Paragraph 4: Talk about some good areas to go out.
- Paragraph 5: Talk about the best time to visit.

C **PERSONAL BEST** Read your partner's description. Choose a paragraph that you like. What do you like about it? Is there a topic sentence? Can you improve the paragraph?

Personal Best Write about your favourite area in your town or city. Why do you like it? What can you do there?

5 and 6 REVIEW and PRACTICE

Grammar

1 Choose the correct options to complete the sentences.

1 I usually work in Budapest, but this month _____ in Prague.
   a I work
   b I working
   c I'm working

2 What _____ at the weekend?
   a do you do
   b you do
   c doing you

3 My father _____ speak three languages.
   a can to
   b can
   c is

4 _____ three people in the picture.
   a They're
   b There are
   c There's

5 The letter M's _____ L and N in the alphabet.
   a between
   b behind
   c under

6 I'm sorry, but I _____ come this evening.
   a am not
   b can't
   c don't

7 _____ a good restaurant near here?
   a Is it
   b There's
   c Is there

8 The books are _____ a shelf in the kitchen.
   a at
   b in
   c on

2 Rewrite the sentences with the tense in brackets.

1 She plays tennis. (present continuous)
   _____
2 They're living in Dubai. (present simple)
   _____
3 What are you doing? (present simple)
   _____
4 We don't work. (present continuous)
   _____
5 Where do you live? (present continuous)
   _____
6 He wears shorts. (present continuous)
   _____
7 She isn't listening. (present simple)
   _____
8 Are you playing tennis? (present simple)
   _____

3 Complete the text using the words in the box.

eat   between   can't   are   on   in   very   can

Inside a luxury plane

This is the Embraer Lineage 1000E. It ¹_____ carry 90 passengers, but this one carries nineteen. There's a living area with leather seats and wool carpets ²_____ the floor. There ³_____ five TVs and four blu-ray players. The seats turn so four people can ⁴_____ around a dining table. The kitchen has two ovens, an espresso machine and a £50,000 dishwasher! There's a ⁵_____ large bed ⁶_____ the bedroom and a shower. There are two toilets and, ⁷_____ the cockpit and the living area, there's another cabin for the crew. For nineteen passengers, there are two flight attendants and two pilots. For luxury you ⁸_____ do better than the Embraer Lineage.

Vocabulary

1 Circle the word that is different. Explain your answer.

1	attic	desk	bathroom	kitchen
2	living room	bedroom	kitchen	apartment
3	sew	cooker	knit	bake
4	boots	shorts	trousers	belt
5	three	second	fourth	first
6	theatre	stadium	concert hall	bridge
7	armchair	cooker	sofa	chair
8	narrow	heavy	modern	wide

REVIEW and PRACTICE 5 and 6

2 Match the definitions 1–8 with the nouns a–h.

1 kitchen furniture with a door where you keep things
2 you put books on these
3 shoes for hot weather or the beach
4 bedroom furniture where you keep clothes
5 a building where you can read and borrow books
6 a room under the house
7 earrings, necklace, etc.
8 where you keep the car

a basement
b library
c wardrobe
d cupboard
e garage
f jewellery
g sandals
h shelves

3 Put the words in the correct columns.

armchair jeans bake hall play chess study
sofa socks kitchen take photos wardrobe
scarf bathroom skirt knit bed

Furniture	Hobbies	Clothes	Rooms

4 Complete the sentences with the words in the box.

department stores bake jeans tie
garden paint shorts monument

1 In my office all the men wear a _____ .
2 I don't like shopping for _____ . I can never find my size.
3 In the park in our town there's a _____ made of stone.
4 At the weekend, I love sitting in our _____ .
5 My wife likes to _____ , in a modern style.
6 I like local shops, but I hate _____ .
7 In the winter, I _____ bread and cakes.
8 I often wear _____ in the summer.

Personal Best

Lesson 5A Describe what you're wearing today.

Lesson 6A Name five rooms in a house.

Lesson 5A Name five other items of clothing.

Lesson 6A Write four sentences about your home, with *there's, there isn't, there are, there aren't*.

Lesson 5C Name three hobbies with the word *play*.

Lesson 6B List four pairs of opposite adjectives.

Lesson 5C List three things you can do well.

Lesson 6C Name four adjectives to describe cities.

Lesson 5C Write three sentences about things you can't do at college or work.

Lesson 6C Write a sentence with *quite* or *really*.

Lesson 5D List three phrases for shopping for clothes.

Lesson 6D Write three sentences to describe your city.

GRAMMAR PRACTICE

1A The verb *be*

We use the verb *be* to say who people are and to give other information about them (for example, where they are from, what job they do, where they are, how they are).

I'm Juan. I'm Mexican.
This is Michel. He's from France.
My sister is a teacher. She's in the classroom.
How are you? I'm fine.

We also use the verb *be* to talk about ages.

I'm 25.

We form negatives with *not* and/or the contraction *n't*, e.g. *am not*, *is not*, *isn't* and *aren't*. We form questions by putting the verb before the subject.

The full forms of the verb *be* are *am*, *is* and *are*. We don't use contractions in short answers.

▶ 1.4	I	he / she / it	you / we / they
+	**I'm** Spanish.	Tom**'s** from Dublin.	You**'re** Japanese.
–	**I'm not** Portuguese.	Maria **isn't** Australian.	We **aren't** from Vietnam.
?	**Am** I from Canada?	**Is** she from New York?	**Are** you from Turkey?
Y/N	Yes, I **am**. / No, I**'m not**.	Yes, she **is**. / No, she **isn't**.	Yes, we **are**. / No, we **aren't**.

We use the contraction *'s* with singular nouns, names and pronouns.

My sister's here.
Sabine's here.
She's here.

We use the contraction *'re* with *you*, *we* and *they*.

You're my friend.
We're Polish.
They're from India.

But we use *are* with plural nouns and names.

My friends are from India.
Gina and Laura are German.

1 Complete the sentences with the correct positive form of the verb *be*.

1 She _____ Brazilian.
2 They _____ from Argentina.
3 Pedro _____ in the classroom.
4 Fabio and Daniele _____ here.
5 I _____ 27.
6 My name _____ Yara.
7 We _____ students.
8 My teachers _____ American.

2 Read the information. Complete the questions and write the short answers (e.g. *Yes, she is*).

Fiona Murray is a student in Montreal, Canada. She's 22 years old. She's from Glasgow in Scotland. Her parents are Scottish.

1 _____ her name Fiona?
_____
2 _____ she 23 years old?
_____
3 _____ she Scottish?
_____
4 _____ she from Montreal?
_____
5 _____ her parents Canadian?
_____
6 _____ her parents from Scotland?
_____

3 Complete the conversation. Use contractions where possible.

A Nice to meet you. My name ¹_____ Carla.
B Nice to meet you, too. I ²_____ William.
A Where ³_____ you from?
B I ⁴_____ from China. ⁵_____ you from Italy?
A No, I ⁶_____ from Italy. I ⁷_____ from Argentina.
B ⁸_____ you here with your family?
A No, I ⁹_____. They ¹⁰_____ at home.

◀ Go back to page 5

1C Possessive adjectives and 's for possession

Possessive adjectives

We use possessive adjectives before nouns to say that something belongs to someone.

It's my wallet.
This is your book.
This is her purse.
Where is his bag?
Is this our umbrella?
This is their car.

▶ 1.12

Subject pronoun	Possessive adjective	
I	my	I'm Spanish. **My** name is Raúl.
you	your	Are **you** ready? **Your** taxi is here.
he	his	**He**'s a great teacher. **His** students are young.
she	her	**She**'s at work, but **her** handbag is at home.
it	its	**It**'s a great city. I like the city for **its** beaches.
we	our	**We**'re from the USA, but **our** son is British.
they	their	**They** aren't here. **Their** train is late.

We use the same possessive adjective for singular and plural nouns.

It's my pen. They're my pens.
This is their car. These are their cars.

's for possession

We add 's to a singular name or noun to say that something belongs to someone.

Tom's book is here.
Where are Lisa's bags?
This is the teacher's desk.

We don't usually use 's to say that something belongs to a thing. We use *of*.

The front of the bus.
The end of the holiday.

With regular plural nouns that end in -s, we use an apostrophe (') after the -s to talk about possession.

These are the students' books.
My friends' names are Lucy and Samir.

With irregular plural nouns, we use 's to talk about possession.

The children's books are in the classroom.
The women's football team are the champions.
Where are the men's bags?

GRAMMAR PRACTICE

1 Choose the correct words to complete the sentences.
1 *She / Her* is 48.
2 *They / Their* names are Maria and Lucy.
3 *Her / She* keys are in the car.
4 I'm *you / your* teacher for today.
5 *We / Our* tickets are in his wallet.
6 *He / His* is from Vietnam.
7 *I / My* surname is Moszkowski.
8 Is *his / he* umbrella black?

2 Complete the sentences with possessive adjectives.
1 Marie and Sylvain are French. _____ family is from Paris.
2 This is _____ wallet. Look, here's your identity card.
3 I am Chinese. _____ family is from Beijing.
4 Italy is famous for _____ food.
5 _____ classmates are from all around the world. We have interesting discussions in class.
6 She's the mum in my host family. _____ name is Tamara.
7 He's my Spanish friend. _____ name is Marcos.
8 What's _____ surname, Megan?

3 Correct and write the statements and questions. Use 's or an apostrophe (') to indicate possession.
1 Are these your sister glasses?
   _____
2 Benedict is Millie boyfriend.
   _____
3 My mothers books are in my bag.
   _____
4 Our teacher name is Susanna.
   _____
5 My parents new car is an Audi.
   _____
6 Our children favourite TV programme is *The Simpsons*.
   _____

◀ Go back to pages 8–9

113

GRAMMAR PRACTICE

2A Present simple: positive and negative

We use the present simple to talk about:

- facts.

I'm Italian.
We live in London.
He doesn't work in a restaurant.

- regular routines.

I work every day.
We go to the cinema at the weekend.
They get up at 10 on Sundays.

We form negatives with *don't/doesn't* + the infinitive of the verb.

▶ 2.3	I / you / we / they	he / she / it
+	We **work** in a hospital.	Laura **works** in an office.
	I **teach** English.	He **teaches** Japanese.
	They **have** a new car.	She **has** a beautiful flat.
	You **make** great coffee.	Simon **makes** good tea.
−	We **don't work** in a school.	Paul **doesn't work** in a shop.
	I **don't teach** French.	He **doesn't teach** in a school.
	They **don't have** a garden.	She **doesn't have** a dog.
	You **don't love** your job.	Damian **doesn't love** his girlfriend.

We usually add *-s* to the infinitive to make the third person singular (*he/she/it*) form.

He serves food in the restaurant.
She loves her job.
Ivan sings at festivals.
Camilla helps her parents at the weekend.

Spelling rules for third person singular (he/she/it)

We usually add *-s* to the infinitive.
work ⇨ works

When the infinitive ends in consonant + *y*, we change the *y* to *i* and then we add *-es*.
study ⇨ studies

When the infinitive ends in *-sh*, *-ch*, *-x* or *-s*, we add *-es*.
finish ⇨ finishes   watch ⇨ watches

Some verbs are irregular.
go ⇨ goes   do ⇨ does   have ⇨ has

---

1 Choose the correct words to complete the sentences.
1. Adam *have / has* a job in a garage.
2. Dean likes Italy, but he *don't / doesn't* like Naples.
3. Tyler *speak / speaks* French, but he doesn't speak German.
4. Carla works in the evening, but she doesn't *work / works* at the weekend.
5. Barbara and Fatima *teach / teaches* Spanish in a college.
6. We *doesn't have / don't have* an office in New York.

2 Complete the sentences with the correct positive form of the verbs in the box.

| watch   serve   start   cut   help   finish   work |
| go   live |

1. I _____ in an apartment in Rio de Janeiro.
2. He's a waiter. He _____ the food.
3. My sister is a hairdresser. She _____ people's hair.
4. They _____ for a bank in the city.
5. Elena _____ tourists. She gives them information.
6. We _____ to work every morning by bus.
7. Karl _____ TV every evening.
8. Sara _____ work at 9 a.m. and she _____ at 5 p.m.

3 Look at the information and complete the positive and negative sentences about Emma.

work: ~~in a hospital~~   in a shop
go to work: ~~by bus~~   by car
finish work: ~~at 4 p.m.~~   at 5.30 p.m.
help: ~~tourists~~   customers

1. Emma _____ in a hospital.
   She _____ in a shop.
2. She _____ by bus.
   She _____ by car.
3. She _____ at 4 p.m.
   She _____ at 5.30 p.m.
4. She _____ tourists.
   She _____ customers.

◀ Go back to page 13

GRAMMAR PRACTICE

2C Present simple: questions

We use questions in the present simple to ask about things that are facts, or regular routines. We form questions in the present simple with *do/does* + subject + infinitive.

Do you like football?
Does she live in a big flat?
Does he work at the weekend?
Do they go out a lot?

We form short answers with *Yes/No*, + subject + *do/does/don't/doesn't*.

Yes, I do.
No, I don't.
Yes, she does.
No, she doesn't

▶ 2.12	I / you / we / they	he / she / it
?	**Do** they **live** in the city?	**Does** he **live** with you?
	Do we **have** more time?	**Does** it **have** a garden?
	Do you **work** in a café?	**Does** she **work** in a hotel?
Y/N	Yes, I **do**. / No, I **don't**.	Yes, she **does**. / No, she **doesn't**.

If we want more information, we put a question word (*what*, *where*, *when*, *why*, *who*, *how*, etc.) before *do/does* at the start of the question.

Where do you live?
Who do you live with?
What does he do at the weekend?
How do you go to work?
When does the class start?
Why do you like football?

1 Put the words in the correct order to make questions.
  1 like / you / do / Spanish / food / ?
  _____
  2 in / Santiago / does / Sandra / live / ?
  _____
  3 they / do / Hong Kong / work / in / ?
  _____
  4 Eric / does / drive / a car / ?
  _____
  5 finish / do / we / at / 5 p.m. / ?
  _____
  6 do / teach / English / you / ?
  _____

2 Look at the short answers to the questions in exercise 1. Correct the mistakes.
  1 Yes, I like. _____
  2 Yes, she do. _____
  3 No, they not. _____
  4 No, he don't drive. _____
  5 Yes, we does. _____
  6 Yes, I teach. _____

3 Write questions.

  1 you / come from Australia
  _____
  2 your flat / have / a TV
  _____
  3 you / like films
  _____
  4 when / you / go to work
  _____
  5 where / your best friend / live
  _____
  6 what / she / do
  _____

◀ Go back to page 17

GRAMMAR PRACTICE

3A Adverbs and expressions of frequency

We use adverbs of frequency with the present simple to talk about routines and how often we do things.

	100%	
always		I always watch TV at the weekend.
usually		I usually read the newspaper at the weekend.
often		I often go for a walk at the weekend.
sometimes		I sometimes study English at the weekend.
hardly ever		I hardly ever drink coffee.
never		I never watch football at the weekend.
	0%	

We usually put adverbs of frequency before the main verb.
I always listen to the radio in the car. NOT ~~Always I listen to the radio in the car~~, or ~~I listen always to the radio in the car~~.

But we usually put adverbs of frequency after the verb *be*.
They're never late. NOT ~~They never are late~~.

We use *How often ... ?* to ask about how frequently actions happen.
How often do you go out for dinner?

We also use expressions of frequency with the present simple to talk about regular habits and routines.
I visit my parents every day.
I visit my grandparents twice a week.
I visit my cousins once a year.

▶ 3.5

I go to the cinema	every once a twice a three times a four times a	day. week. month. year.

Once means 'one time' and *twice* means 'two times'.

We usually use expressions of frequency at the end of a sentence. We sometimes use them at the start of a sentence.
I visit my cousins once a year.
Once a year, I visit my cousins.
NOT ~~I once a year visit my cousins~~.

1 Rewrite the sentences. Put the adverbs of frequency in the correct places.
  1 My father reads the newspaper. (always)
  _____
  2 My aunt has lunch with friends. (often)
  _____
  3 My cousin is at home in the evening. (usually)
  _____
  4 They work at the weekend. (sometimes)
  _____
  5 I go to the cinema. (never)
  _____
  6 I'm very busy. (often)
  _____

2 Complete the sentences. Put one word in each sentence.

  1 I go to the gym _____ day.
  2 We go on holiday three times a _____ – in March, May and October.
  3 I see my grandparents twice _____ week.
  4 I usually have a cup of coffee _____ a day – with breakfast and after lunch.
  5 My dad plays golf three _____ a week.
  6 My brother visits me twice a week, but my sister only visits me _____ a week.

3 Correct the sentences.
  1 Never Sam listens to music.
  _____
  2 The flats here usually are nice.
  _____
  3 We eat out hardly ever on Saturdays.
  _____
  4 Lidia drives to work every days.
  _____
  5 We see our cousins four or five times year.
  _____
  6 I go to the theatre once time a month.
  _____

◀ Go back to page 23

GRAMMAR PRACTICE

3C love, like, hate, enjoy, don't mind + noun/-ing form

We use *love, like, hate, enjoy* and *don't mind* to say if we feel positively or negatively about something.

The verbs *love, like* and *enjoy* have a positive meaning.
I love tennis. ☺☺
I like basketball. ☺
I enjoy swimming. ☺

The verb *don't mind* has a neutral meaning.
I don't mind working at the weekend. 😐
Soraya doesn't mind cats. 😐

The verbs *don't like/don't enjoy* and *hate* have a negative meaning.
I don't like going to the gym. ☹
Emil hates watching football. ☹☹

We use a noun or the *-ing* form of a verb after these verbs.

▶ 3.9

I love	tennis. / playing tennis.
I enjoy	museums. / visiting museums.
I like	dogs. / walking my dog.
I don't mind	rock music. / listening to rock music.
I don't like	Indian food. / eating Indian food.
I hate	football. / watching football.

Spelling rules for the -ing form

We usually add *-ing* to the infinitive of the verb.
play ⇨ *playing*   *talk* ⇨ *talking*

When a one-syllable infinitive ends in consonant + *e*, we usually remove the *e* and then add *-ing*.
take ⇨ *taking*   *live* ⇨ *living*
BUT *be* ⇨ *being*

When a one-syllable infinitive ends in a vowel + a consonant, we double the consonant and then add *-ing*.
sit ⇨ *sitting*   *plan* ⇨ *planning*

When an infinitive ends with a vowel *l*, we double the *l*.
travel ⇨ *travelling*

1 Complete the sentences with the *-ing* form of the verb in brackets.
   1 They like _____ new places. (visit)
   2 I like _____ time with my family. (spend)
   3 He doesn't like _____. (swim)
   4 She hates _____ dinner. (make)
   5 Does Freya like _____? (drive)
   6 I love _____ on the beach. (run)
   7 Do you like _____ a student? (be)
   8 My parents love _____ photos. (take)

2 Complete the sentences with *love, like, don't mind, don't like, hate* and the *-ing* form of the verbs in the box.

   | work   go   meet   play   make   cook   learn   listen |

   1 They ☺ _____ Japanese food.
   2 Sadiq ☺ _____ in a bank.
   3 I ☹ _____ French.
   4 Tania ☺☺ _____ clothes.
   5 I ☺ _____ my friends in town.
   6 We ☹☹ _____ golf.
   7 Liam ☺ _____ shopping.
   8 I ☺ _____ to the radio.

3 Read the sentences. Tick (✓) the ones that are correct. Rewrite the incorrect ones.
   1 I love American films. ☐
   _____
   2 Do you like cook? ☐
   _____
   3 Pedro doesn't like rugby. ☐
   _____
   4 I hate be late. ☐
   _____
   5 Tomiko enjoys to play football. ☐
   _____
   6 I love talking to my friends. ☐
   _____

◀ Go back to page 27

GRAMMAR PRACTICE

4A Prepositions of time

We use different prepositions to make common time expressions.

▶ 4.2

Preposition	We use this with ...	Example
in	*the* + parts of the day	in the morning(s) in the afternoon(s) in the evening(s)
	the + seasons	in the winter in the spring in the summer in the autumn
	months of the year	in January in September
on	days of the week	on Monday(s) on Tuesday(s)
	days and parts of the day	on Thursday morning(s) on Saturday night(s) on Friday evening(s) on New Year's Day
at	times	at 6 o'clock at 11.30
	midnight/midday/night	at midnight at midday at night
	the weekend	at the weekend
	festivals	at Christmas at New Year
from ... to	days	from Wednesday to Sunday
	months	from January to June
	times	from 6.30 to 9.00
	years	from 2000 to 2006

Look! *at night* NOT ~~*in the night*~~ BUT *on Friday night*

We use these time expressions at the start or at the end of a sentence. We use a comma after them if they are at the start.

I usually get up at 7.30.
At 7.30, I usually get up.
I have an Italian class on Wednesday evening.
On Wednesday evening, I have an Italian class.

We can use plurals for days, parts of the day and *weekend* if we talk about things that we do regularly.

I don't work at the weekend / at weekends.
In the morning / In the mornings, I often go for a run before work.

1 Complete the sentences with *in*, *on*, *at* or *from ... to*.
   1 I usually have a shower _____ the evening.
   2 Conor does his homework _____ night.
   3 I'm at work _____ 8.30 _____ 6.30 every day.
   4 They visit their cousins _____ Christmas.
   5 We always go out _____ Friday nights.
   6 Is it hot here _____ August?
   7 The days are short _____ the winter.
   8 What do you like doing _____ the weekend?

2 Read the text and <u>underline</u> eight mistakes. Write the correct prepositions below the text.

Every day, from Monday in Friday, I get up at 6.30. I leave the house at 7.30 and I start working on 8.15. I don't work on Friday afternoons. I finish work in midday.

On July and August, it's very hot. I usually go to the swimming pool with my children in the afternoons, and in night, we go for a walk.

In the weekend, I don't get up early. At Saturday mornings, I go for a run on 11, and then my wife and I make lunch. On Sundays, we usually take the children to visit my parents or my wife's parents.

1 _____   4 _____   7 _____
2 _____   5 _____   8 _____
3 _____   6 _____

3 Write sentences. Add prepositions.
   1 I visit my grandparents / the weekend
   _____
   2 February / we usually go skiing
   _____
   3 I usually stop for a cup of tea / midday
   _____
   4 Wednesday evenings / my sister does yoga
   _____
   5 Carlos works / Monday / Saturday
   _____
   6 My daughter's birthday is / the spring
   _____

◀ Go back to page 31

118

4C Present continuous

We use the present continuous to talk about:

- things that are happening now.

I'm having a shower.
It's raining.
What are you reading?

- things that are temporary.

We're staying in a hotel.
I'm not working this week.

We form the present continuous with the verb *be* + the *-ing* form of the main verb.

▶ 4.9	I	he / she / it	you / we / they
+	I'm getting dressed.	He's getting dressed.	We're getting dressed.
−	I'm not watching TV.	She isn't watching TV.	We aren't watching TV.
?	Am I sleeping?	Is she sleeping?	Are they sleeping?
Y/N	Yes, I am. / No, I'm not.	Yes, she is. / No, she isn't.	Yes, they are. / No, they aren't.

Spelling rules for the *-ing* form

We usually add *-ing* to the infinitive of the verb.

play ⇨ playing   talk ⇨ talking

When an infinitive ends in consonant + *e*, we usually remove the *e* and then add *-ing*.

take ⇨ taking   live ⇨ living
BUT be ⇨ being

When a one-syllable infinitive ends in a vowel + a consonant, we double the consonant and then add *-ing*.

sit ⇨ sitting   plan ⇨ planning

When an infinitive ends with a vowel *l*, we double the *l*.

travel ⇨ travelling

Look! We often use the present continuous with time expressions such as (*right*) *now*, *today*, *this week/month/year* and *at the moment*.
I'm having breakfast at the moment.
I'm studying a lot this month.

GRAMMAR PRACTICE

1 Put the words in the correct order to make sentences.

1 using / the computer / Ella / is / ?
_____
2 parents / I / visiting / am / my
_____
3 reading / Matt / the newspaper / is
_____
4 isn't / my / working / phone
_____
5 staying / we / are / in a hotel / this weekend
_____
6 you / going / where / are / ?
_____

2 Complete the sentences with the correct present continuous forms of the verbs in brackets.

1 I _____ dinner at the moment. (have)
2 We _____ to the beach right now. (go)
3 The internet _____ today. (not work)
4 _____ Tim _____ a shower? (have)
5 She _____ a taxi home. (get)
6 What _____ you _____? (do)
7 I _____ today because it's Saturday. (not study)
8 _____ I _____ in the right place? (sit)

3 Look at the picture. Use the words to make questions and write true short answers.

1 they / talk
_____
2 they / have / a good time
_____
3 it / snow
_____
4 it / rain
_____
5 she / carry / an umbrella
_____
6 he / wear / glasses
_____

◀ Go back to page 35

GRAMMAR PRACTICE

5A Present simple and present continuous

We use the present simple to talk about facts and things which happen regularly.

Sam lives in Australia.
We wear a uniform at work.
I usually wake up at six o'clock.

We use the present continuous to talk about things that are happening now, or are temporary.

I'm wearing blue trousers today.
I'm going to work by car today.
My friend is living in London at the moment.

We often use the present simple and present continuous together to contrast the usual situation and what is happening now, or is temporary.

▶ 5.2 Present simple and present continuous

It **doesn't usually** rain in the summer,	but it**'s raining** today.
I usually wear jeans to work,	but today I**'m wearing** a suit.
I don't often cook,	but I**'m cooking** every evening this week.

There are some verbs that describe a state, not an action. We don't normally use these verbs in the present continuous.

I prefer this music. NOT *I'm preferring this music.*
Sorry, I don't understand. NOT *Sorry, I'm not understanding.*
I have some new sandals. NOT *I'm having some new sandals.*

> **Look!** Here are some common state verbs:
> Feelings: like, love, hate, want, prefer, need.
> Thoughts and opinions: know, believe, remember, forget, understand, think
> States: be, belong, have (when we talk about relationships or possessions).

---

1 Choose the correct words to complete the sentences and questions.
1. What *do you do* / *are you doing* at the moment?
2. *Is he going* / *Does he go* there often?
3. They*'re working* / *work* late tonight.
4. I *never read* / *'m never reading* books.
5. I*'m studying* / *study* in my bedroom now.
6. Most people *finish* / *are finishing* school at eighteen or nineteen years old.

2 Complete the sentences with the present simple or present continuous form of the verbs in brackets.
1. I _____ right now. (read)
2. He _____ to New York three times a year. (go)
3. They _____ us every summer. (visit)
4. How _____ Erica _____ to work today? (get)
5. I _____ coffee very often. (not drink)
6. We _____ a really good TV series at the moment. (watch)
7. I usually _____ juice for breakfast. (have)
8. Please be quiet – the baby _____. (sleep)

3 Read the information. Then complete the text about Jan.

Jan usually ¹_____ tea and toast for breakfast. He ²_____ a suit. He ³_____ all day. This week, Jan is on holiday. He ⁴_____ coffee and croissants for breakfast. He ⁵_____ shorts and a T-shirt. He ⁶_____ a great time!

120

◀ Go back to page 41

GRAMMAR PRACTICE

5C can and can't

We use *can* and *can't* to talk about:

- ability.
I can swim.
My brother can play the guitar.
I can't speak Italian.
My sister can't cook.

- possibility.
You can make money from your hobby.
It can snow here in the winter.
You can't get there by bus.

- permission.
You can take my umbrella.
We can sit here.
We can't park in this street.
You can't use this gym if you aren't a member.

To make questions with *can*, we put *can* before the subject. We use the same form for all people.

5.8 I / you / he / she / it / we / they

+	I **can play** the piano.
	They **can go** to the city by bus.
	We **can finish** work early today.
−	She **can't speak** Japanese.
	They **can't work** at night.
	You **can't walk** on the grass.
?	**Can** she **play** the guitar?
	Can you **come** to my party?
	Can we **park** the car here?
Y/N	Yes, we **can**. / No, we **can't**.

Look! The full form of *can't* is *cannot*. We don't often use *cannot*; *can't* is the usual negative form.
I can't meet you tonight. NOT *I cannot meet you tonight.*

---

1 Look at the table and complete the sentences with *can* or *can't*.

	Craig	Helen	Manuel	Silvia
cook	✔	✔	✘	✔
play tennis	✔	✘	✔	✘
drive	✔	✔	✔	✘
speak French	✘	✘	✘	✔

1 Craig _____ cook, but he _____ speak French.
2 Helen _____ play tennis, but she _____ drive.
3 Craig, Helen and Manuel _____ speak French.
4 Manuel _____ cook, but he _____ drive.
5 Silvia _____ cook and speak French.
6 Craig, Helen and Manuel _____ drive.

2 Write short answers to the questions about the people in exercise 1.

1 Can Silvia drive? _____
2 Can Craig play tennis? _____
3 Can Helen cook? _____
4 Can Manuel speak French? _____
5 Can Helen and Silvia play tennis? _____
6 Can Craig and Manuel drive? _____

3 Complete the sentences about the pictures. Use *can* or *can't* and the phrases in the box.

> walk on the grass   cycle in this street
> pay with a credit card   park here for one hour

1 You _____
2 You _____
3 You _____
4 You _____

◀ Go back to page 45

GRAMMAR PRACTICE

6A there is/there are, some/any, prepositions of place

We use *there is* to say that something singular exists.

There's a sofa in the living room.
There's a small balcony in my flat.

We use *there are* for the plural form.

There are five people in my family.
There are three bedrooms in her flat.

We use *some* and *any* with plural nouns. We use *some* in positive sentences when more than one thing or person exists, but we don't say exactly how many.

There are some chairs in the classroom.
There are some new students in our class.
I have some books in my bag.

We use *any* in negative sentences and questions with plural nouns.

There aren't any tables.
I don't have any brothers or sisters.
Are there any shelves in the bedroom?

▶ 6.3	Singular nouns	Plural nouns
+	**There's** a shelf in my bedroom.	**There are some** shelves in the kitchen.
–	**There isn't** a chair in my bedroom.	**There aren't any** chairs in the kitchen.
?	**Is there** a cupboard in your bedroom?	**Are there any** cupboards in the kitchen?
Y/N	Yes, **there is.** / No, **there isn't.**	Yes, **there are.** / No, **there aren't.**

Prepositions of place

▶ 6.7 We use prepositions of place to describe location.

The window is opposite the door.

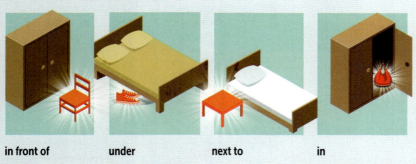

in front of   under   next to   in

on   between   behind   opposite

---

1 Read the advertisement and then complete the sentences with *there is/are* and *there isn't/aren't*.

> Third-floor two-bedroom flat in a popular area near shops and a park. Five minutes' walk to Holborn Road underground station. Living room with big windows. Kitchen, bathroom (shower only, no bath). Empty – ready to move in!

1 _____ two bedrooms.
2 _____ a bathroom.
3 _____ a garden, but _____ a park near the flat.
4 _____ some big windows in the living room.
5 _____ a bath in the bathroom.
6 _____ any people in the flat at the moment.
7 _____ some shops near the flat.
8 _____ an underground station near the flat.

2 Complete the questions and answers about a flat.

1 _____ garage with your flat?
   No, _____.
2 _____ shelves in the living room?
   Yes, _____.
3 _____ basement that you can use?
   Yes, _____.
4 _____ sofa in the living room?
   Yes, _____.
5 _____ good restaurants in the area?
   No, _____.
6 _____ schools for the children?
   Yes, _____.

3 Look at the floor plan of a house. Complete the sentences with prepositions of place.

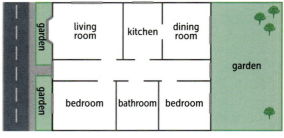

1 The kitchen is _____ the bathroom.
2 The bathroom is _____ the two bedrooms.
3 The dining room is _____ the kitchen.
4 There is a small garden _____ the house.
5 There is a large garden _____ the house.
6 There are some trees _____ the large garden.

◀ Go back to page 49

6C Modifiers

We use modifiers with adjectives to make them stronger or weaker.

It's really/very big.

It's quite big.

It isn't very big.

It isn't big at all.

We use *really* and *very* to make an adjective stronger.
The city is really big.
The market is very busy on Saturdays.

We use *quite* and *not very* to make an adjective weaker. If we use *quite*, the adjective is correct but weaker. If we use *not very*, the adjective has the opposite meaning.
The bridge is quite old.
The flat isn't very old. = The flat is quite new.

We use *not* + adjective + *at all* to give a strong opposite meaning to an adjective.
The beach isn't crowded at all. = The beach is very empty.
The restaurant isn't expensive at all. = The restaurant is very cheap.

If we are modifying an adjective before a singular noun, we put *quite* before *a/an*. Other modifiers go after *a/an*.

▶ 6.12

modifier + adjective	modifier + adjective + (singular) noun
The house is **really/very beautiful**.	It's a **really/very beautiful** house.
The house is **quite** beautiful.	It's **quite** a **beautiful** house.
The house is**n't very** beautiful.	It is**n't** a **very beautiful** house.
The house is**n't beautiful at all**.	It is**n't** a **beautiful** house **at all**.

GRAMMAR PRACTICE

1 Rewrite the sentences. Put the modifier in brackets in the correct place.
 1 The beach is busy today. (very)
 _____
 2 The stadium is full at the moment. (not very)
 _____
 3 You can buy beautiful presents at the market. (really)
 _____
 4 This is an old apartment block. (quite)
 _____
 5 This café is expensive. (not … at all)
 _____
 6 I'm reading an interesting book at the moment. (quite)
 _____

2 Put the words in the correct order to make sentences.
 1 a / bathroom / there / large / is / quite
 _____
 2 a / skyscraper / I / in / really / tall / work
 _____
 3 I / road / on / a / live / quiet / very
 _____
 4 clothes / are / these / very / expensive
 _____
 5 sister / at / isn't / my / busy / all
 _____
 6 food / nice / the / isn't / very
 _____

3 Look at Andy's review of his holiday. Complete the sentences about it using modifiers and the adjectives in brackets.

The old town is ¹_____really beautiful_____ (beautiful), but it's ²_____ (busy). The restaurants are ³_____ (expensive) and the food is ⁴_____ (good). The beaches are ⁵_____ (crowded), but they're ⁶_____ (clean). It's ⁷_____ (good) place for families because it's ⁸_____ (cheap) place to stay.

◀ Go back to page 53

VOCABULARY PRACTICE

1A Countries and nationalities

1 ▶ 1.2 Complete the table with the nationalities in the box. Listen and check.

> Portuguese   British   Mexican   French   Argentinian
> Polish   Chinese   Italian   Brazilian   Spanish

Country	Nationality
1 China	_____
2 Japan	Japanese
3 Portugal	_____
4 Vietnam	Vietnamese
5 England	English
6 Ireland	Irish
7 Poland	_____
8 Scotland	Scottish
9 Spain	_____
10 Sweden	Swedish
11 Turkey	Turkish
12 the UK	_____
13 Germany	German
14 Mexico	_____
15 the USA	American
16 Argentina	_____
17 Australia	Australian
18 Brazil	_____
19 Canada	Canadian
20 Egypt	Egyptian
21 Italy	_____
22 Russia	Russian
23 France	_____
24 Wales	Welsh

2 Complete the sentences about the people.
1 Ewan is Scottish. He's from _____.
2 Natasha is Russian. She's from _____.
3 Troy is American. He's from _____.
4 Mesut is Turkish. He's from _____.
5 Dominique and Ellie are Canadian. They're from _____.
6 Laura is Welsh. She's from _____.
7 Maciek and Janusz are Polish. They're from _____.
8 Hong is Vietnamese. She's from _____.
9 Oscar and Ana are Brazilian. They're from _____.
10 José Carlos is Mexican. He's from _____.

1A Numbers 1–1,000

1 ▶ 1.7 Write the missing numbers. Listen and check.

0 zero/nought	21 twenty-one
1 one	22 twenty-two
2 two	23 _____
3 three	30 thirty
4 four	31 _____
5 five	32 thirty-two
6 six	40 forty
7 seven	50 _____
8 eight	60 sixty
9 nine	70 seventy
10 ten	80 eighty
11 _____	90 ninety
12 twelve	100 a hundred/one hundred
13 thirteen	101 a hundred and one
14 fourteen	102 _____
15 _____	200 two hundred
16 sixteen	210 two hundred and ten
17 seventeen	322 _____
18 eighteen	468 four hundred and sixty-eight
19 nineteen	713 _____
20 _____	1,000 a thousand/one thousand

2 Look at the pictures and complete the numbers in words.

1 It's Lucy's birthday. She's _____.

5 A normal year has _____ days.

2 The Jones family live at _____, Main Street.

6 It's _____ kilometres to Paris.

3 The population of Newtown is _____.

7 Our hotel room is number _____.

4 The bike is _____ pounds.

8 The watch is _____ euros.

◀ Go back to page 4   ◀ Go back to page 5

VOCABULARY PRACTICE

1C Personal objects

1 ▶1.9 Match the words in the box with the pictures 1–20. Listen and check.

| key sunglasses mirror gloves chewing gum torch tissues photo stamps glasses |
| identity card watch umbrella hairbrush wallet sweets purse comb tablet phone |

1 _____ 2 _____ 3 _____ 4 _____ 5 _____

6 _____ 7 _____ 8 _____ 9 _____ 10 _____

11 _____ 12 _____ 13 _____ 14 _____ 15 _____

16 _____ 17 _____ 18 _____ 19 _____ 20 _____

2 Read the information about plurals. Write plurals for the words.

> **Look!** We make most plurals by adding *-s* or *-es*. We add *-es* if a word ends in *-ch, -sh, -s,-x* or *-z*:
> *stamp* ⇨ *stamps*, *watch* ⇨ *watches*.

1 comb _____
2 hairbrush _____
3 card _____
4 key _____
5 mirror _____
6 phone _____
7 photo _____
8 purse _____
9 tablet _____
10 torch _____
11 umbrella _____
12 wallet _____

3 Choose the correct words to complete the sentences.

1 Is that rain? Where's my *umbrella* / *hairbrush*?
2 Look at this *photo* / *mirror* of my boyfriend.
3 Do you have a *tablet* / *stamp*? I want to send a letter.
4 What's the time? I don't have my *wallet* / *watch*.
5 It's very cold today. Take some *purses* / *gloves* with you.
6 I always wear *combs* / *glasses* when I read.
7 Where's my car *key* / *card*?
8 I have twenty euros in my *purse* / *torch*.
9 It's very sunny. Where are my *tablets* / *sunglasses*?
10 *Chewing gum is* / *Sweets are* bad for your teeth.

4 ▶1.10 Now read about the pronunciation of plurals ending in *-s* and *-es*. Put the plurals from exercise 2 into the table. Listen and check.

/s/	/z/	/ɪz/
when the final sound in the word is /t/, /k/, /p/, /f/ or /θ/	when the final sound in the word is /b/, /d/, /g/, /l/, /m/, /n/, /v/, /ð/ or a vowel sound	when the final sound in the word is /tʃ/, /dʒ/, /ʒ/, /ʃ/, /s/, /ks/ or /z/
	combs	

◀ Go back to page 8

137

VOCABULARY PRACTICE

2A Jobs and job verbs

1 ▶ 2.1 Match the jobs in the box with the pictures 1–20. Listen and check.

| hairdresser   tour guide   police officer   doctor   electrician   teacher   taxi driver   dentist   flight attendant   singer   mechanic |
| nurse   lawyer   waiter/waitress   receptionist   businessman/businesswoman   accountant   builder   chef   shop assistant |

1 _____

2 _____

3 _____

4 _____

5 _____

6 _____

7 _____

8 _____

9 _____

10 _____

11 _____

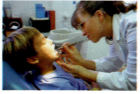
12 _____

13 _____

14 _____

15 _____

16 _____

17 _____

18 _____

19 _____

20 _____

2 ▶ 2.2 Match the halves to make sentences. Listen and check.

1 He cooks
2 He drives
3 He repairs
4 They make
5 She serves
6 He wears
7 They start
8 She teaches
9 He finishes
10 He cuts
11 She helps
12 She sells

a a taxi.
b food in a restaurant.
c English in a school.
d work at 9 a.m.
e people's hair.
f food to customers.
g people at a tourist office.
h cars in a garage.
i computers in a shop.
j a suit at work.
k clothes in a factory.
l work at 6 p.m.

3 Complete the sentences with job verbs and jobs.

1 Mario works in a garage. He _____ cars. He's a _____.
2 Samantha works in a secondary school. She _____ French and Spanish. She's a _____.
3 Hitoshi and Kazuo work in the kitchen of a restaurant. They _____ the food for the customers. They are _____.
4 Tomiko also works in the restaurant. She _____ the customers in the restaurant. She's a _____.
5 Maya is a _____. She _____ people's hair.
6 Terry works at night. He _____ a taxi in different places in Liverpool. He's a _____.
7 Raul works in a clothes shop. He _____ clothes. He's a _____.
8 Ola, Piotr and Marta are in a pop group. Marta plays the drums, Piotr plays the guitar, and Ola _____. She's the group's _____.
9 Mark works on aeroplanes. He _____ a uniform. He _____ food and drink to the passengers. He's a _____.
10 Clara works in a hospital. She _____ work at 7 p.m. and she _____ late, at 8.30 p.m. She isn't a doctor. She's a _____.

◀ Go back to page 13

VOCABULARY PRACTICE

2B Activities (1)

1 ▶ 2.7 Look at pictures 1–20 and complete the phrases with the words in the box. Listen and check.

| study | book | (my) friends | read | time | walk | guitar | cinema | TV |
| dinner | watch | play | radio | listen | run | coffee | film | relax |

1 go to the _____   2 go out for _____   3 go for a _____   4 go for a _____   5 go for a _____   6 _____ to music

7 listen to the _____   8 spend _____ with my family   9 _____ tennis   10 play the _____   11 _____ the newspaper   12 read a _____

13 _____   14 see a _____   15 _____   16 meet _____   17 _____ football   18 watch _____

2 Complete the sentences with phrases from exercise 1. Use the correct form.
1 My brother _____ in a band. He's really good.
2 My dad always _____ at breakfast. He likes reading the sports pages.
3 We _____ on Saturday evenings. We go to a very good Chinese restaurant.
4 I want to do some exercise. Do you want to _____ with me in the park?
5 I _____ all the time. I'm a Barcelona fan.
6 I _____ in the car. I play my favourite songs.
7 After work on Fridays, I _____ in town and we go to a café to chat.
8 At the weekend, Rosie _____: her parents, her brother and her two sisters.
9 My sister and I _____ on Saturdays. I usually have a cappuccino and she has a latte.
10 I _____ in the library after university classes.

3 Correct the mistakes in the sentences. Rewrite the sentences.
1 My friend Tara plays a guitar in a rock group.
   _____
2 Do you want to look a film tonight?
   _____
3 I always listen music on the train.
   _____
4 I usually meet the friends after work.
   _____
5 I want to go the cinema this weekend.
   _____
6 My parents play the tennis with their friends.
   _____

◀ Go back to page 14

139

VOCABULARY PRACTICE

3A Family

1 ▶ 3.2 Complete Jack's family tree with the words in the box. Listen and check.

| wife father-in-law sister-in-law daughter brother sister nephew niece father aunt cousin (×2) grandmother |

Bill – ¹grandfather
Marion – 2 _____

Diane – 3 _____
Robert – 4 _____
Christine – ⁵mother-in-law
Harry – 6 _____
Jane – ⁷mother
Tim – ⁸uncle

Stephen – 9 _____
Paula – 10 _____
Louise – 11 _____
Carrie – 12 _____
JACK
Andy – 13 _____
Sian – 14 _____
David – ¹⁵brother-in-law

Evie – 16 _____
Zach – ¹⁷son
Solomon – 18 _____
Carmen – 19 _____

2 ▶ 3.3 Complete the sentences with the correct names.
1 _____ and _____ are Jack's parents.
2 _____ and _____ are Jack's parents-in-law.
3 _____ and _____ are Jack's grandparents.
4 _____ and _____ are Jack's children.
5 _____, _____, _____ and _____ are Harry and Jane's grandchildren.
6 Jack is _____ and _____'s son-in-law.
7 Carrie is _____ and _____'s daughter-in-law.
8 Jack is _____'s husband.
9 _____, _____ and _____ are Bill and Marion's grandsons.
10 _____ is Robert and Christine's granddaughter.

3 Complete the table with the family words from exercises 1 and 2.

male	female	male and female

4 Find three false definitions. Write the correct definitions.
1 My nephew is my brother's son. _____
2 My mother-in-law is my wife's sister. _____
3 My daughter is my son's sister. _____
4 My granddaughter is my daughter's daughter. _____
5 My niece is my cousin's daughter. _____
6 My father-in-law is my husband's father. _____
7 My grandparents are my nephew's parents. _____
8 My cousins are my aunt's children. _____

◀ Go back to page 23

VOCABULARY PRACTICE

3C Activities (2)

1 ▶ 3.7 Match the phrases below with the pictures a–p. Listen and check.

do	play	go	have	visit
1 karate ___	3 golf ___	6 bowling ___	11 a barbecue ___	14 a gallery ___
2 yoga ___	4 volleyball ___	7 cycling ___	12 a picnic ___	15 a museum ___
	5 the violin ___	8 dancing ___	13 a takeaway ___	16 relatives ___
		9 shopping ___		
		10 swimming ___		

2 Complete the sentences with the verbs in the correct form.
 1 They _____ a barbecue every time it's hot and sunny.
 2 We always _____ a picnic for my birthday.
 3 I _____ yoga on Friday mornings.
 4 We _____ volleyball on the beach.
 5 I sometimes _____ galleries.
 6 I always _____ a takeaway with my family on Saturday evenings.
 7 My son _____ the violin in his school orchestra.
 8 I don't go to the gym, but I _____ dancing at the weekend.
 9 My best friend _____ cycling every Sunday afternoon.
 10 My children often _____ bowling with their friends.

3 Write the phrases from exercise 1 that match the sentences.
 1 If you're interested in very old things, you can do this.
   _____
 2 This is when you go to see your cousins, grandparents, etc.
   _____
 3 Lots of people do this Japanese sport.
   _____
 4 Lots of people do this sport on the beach in summer.
   _____
 5 You can do this in the sea or at a pool.
   _____
 6 This is when you cook a meal outside.
   _____
 7 You need a bicycle for this.
   _____
 8 You need a very large open green space if you want to do this sport.
   _____

◀ Go back to page 26

VOCABULARY PRACTICE

4A Daily routine verbs

1 ▶ 4.1 Match the pictures a–o with the activities 1–15. Listen and check.

1 have lunch ____
2 have dinner ____
3 go to school ____
4 get dressed ____
5 wake up ____
6 have a shower ____
7 get up ____
8 go to work ____
9 have a bath ____
10 go to bed ____
11 go to sleep ____
12 leave school ____
13 get home ____
14 leave work ____
15 have breakfast ____

a
b
c
d
e
f
g
h
i
j
k
l
m
n
o

◀ Go back to page 30

4B The weather and the seasons

1 ▶ 4.5 Look at the pictures and complete the sentences with the cities. Listen and check.

 22° BARCELONA
 -11° ST PETERSBURG
 14° SHANGHAI
 36° MUMBAI
 12° SAN FRANCISCO
 10° LIVERPOOL
 1° STOCKHOLM

1 It's raining/rainy in _____.
2 It's snowing/snowy in _____.
3 It's hot in _____.
4 It's warm in _____.
5 It's very cold in _____.
6 It's wet in _____.
7 It's sunny in _____.
8 It's foggy in _____.
9 It's windy in _____.
10 It's cloudy in _____.
11 It's icy in _____.
12 It's cold in _____.

2 Label the pictures with the seasons. Then write a word from exercise 1 to describe the weather in each season.

summer   autumn   spring   winter

_____, _____   _____, _____   _____, _____   _____, _____

◀ Go back to page 32

142

VOCABULARY PRACTICE

5A Clothes

1 ▶ 5.1 Label the clothes and the jewellery in the pictures with the words in the box. Listen and check.

| belt tie necklace bracelet trousers T-shirt earrings boots coat jacket jeans sandals top
trainers scarf jewellery dress gloves hat shirt shoes shorts skirt socks suit jumper |

2 Choose the correct words to complete the sentences.
1 My trousers are too big. I need a *necklace / belt*.
2 Jim hates wearing a suit and *tie / scarf*. He prefers jeans and a T-shirt.
3 When Anna goes running, she wears *boots / trainers*.
4 I like wearing jewellery, especially *sandals / earrings*.
5 It's cold outside. Wear a scarf and *gloves / shorts*.
6 My daughter likes climbing trees so she wears *trousers / a skirt*.
7 Sally's going to a party so she's wearing a *T-shirt / dress*.
8 In the summer, I like wearing *shorts / shoes* and sandals.
9 Shall I wear my red *top / socks* or my blue jumper with my jeans?
10 You need to wear a *coat / suit* when you go to a job interview.

◀ Go back to page 40

5A Ordinal numbers

1 ▶ 5.4 Write the ordinal numbers. Listen and check.

1 first
2 _____
3 third
4 _____
5 _____
6 sixth
7 seventh

8 _____
9 _____
10 tenth
11 _____
12 _____
13 thirteenth
14 fourteenth

15 _____
20 twentieth
21 _____
22 twenty-second
30 thirtieth
40 _____
50 fiftieth

2 Complete the sentences with the ordinal numbers in brackets. Write them in words.
1 Kazakhstan is the _____ biggest country in the world. (9th)
2 December is the _____ month of the year. (12th)
3 Barack Obama was the _____ president of the USA. (44th)
4 International Women's Day is the _____ of March. (8th)
5 Valentine's Day is on the _____ of February. (14th)
6 St Andrew's Day is the _____ of November. (30th)

◀ Go back to page 41

143

VOCABULARY PRACTICE

5C Hobbies

1 ▶ 5.7 Match the verbs in the box with the pictures 1–15. You need some verbs more than once. Listen and check.

collect play make sew knit sing dance take write paint draw bake

1 _____

2 _____

3 _____ online games

4 _____

5 _____ photos

6 _____ a blog

7 _____ the drums

8 _____ jewellery

9 _____

10 _____ chess

11 _____

12 _____

13 _____ stamps

14 _____

15 _____ coins

2 Match the hobbies with the descriptions.
1 These hobbies are connected to music.
   _____
2 People often do these hobbies in beautiful places.
   _____
3 This hobby is connected to food.
   _____
4 You study and collect objects for this hobby.
   _____
5 You need another person to do this hobby.
   _____
6 These hobbies are connected to clothes.
   _____
7 You need to use the internet for this hobby.
   _____

3 Choose the correct words to complete the sentences.
1 At the moment, I'm *drawing* / *knitting* a jumper. I want to finish it before the winter.
2 I collect *stamps* / *coins*. My favourite one is made of gold.
3 Everyone can *sew* / *take photos* on their smartphones, but some people can do it really well.
4 My friend Emily *makes* / *sews* jewellery. She's making me a necklace for my birthday.
5 We need someone who *plays the drums* / *bakes* for our band. Do you know anyone?
6 My cousin is travelling in Africa at the moment, and she *makes* / *writes* a blog every day. I like reading it to find out what she's doing.
7 My wife loves *painting* / *baking* and I love eating her cakes and biscuits. We're a perfect match!
8 My friend Matt is learning to *dance* / *sing*. At the moment, he's learning the Tango.

144   ◀ Go back to page 44

VOCABULARY PRACTICE

6A Rooms and furniture

1 ▶ 6.1 Label the picture with the rooms and places in the box. Listen and check.

| garden | balcony | kitchen | bedroom | living room | bathroom | dining room | study | garage | hall | toilet | attic | basement | stairs |

2 ▶ 6.2 Find the furniture items in the picture. Write the letters a-l. Listen and check.

1 armchair _____   4 cooker _____   7 shelves _____   9 table _____   11 washing machine _____
2 bed _____   5 cupboard _____   8 sofa _____   10 wardrobe _____   12 mirror _____
3 chairs _____   6 desk _____

◀ Go back to page 48

6B Common adjectives

1 ▶ 6.8 Match the adjectives with their opposites. Listen and check.

1 expensive   a wide
2 clean   b uncomfortable
3 narrow   c light
4 noisy   d cheap
5 comfortable   e traditional
6 heavy   f dirty
7 modern   g quiet

2 Complete the sentences with opposite adjectives.

1 I don't like _____ bars and restaurants. I like _____ places where you can talk with friends.
2 My girlfriend usually buys _____ clothes. I'm different – I buy _____ clothes and have some money for other things.
3 We have two sofas. One is old, but very _____ – it's perfect for watching a film. The other one is new, but it's _____.
4 My husband wants to buy some _____ furniture, but I don't. I want some _____ things because our apartment is very new.
5 Your T-shirt is really _____! Go and find a _____ top.
6 My bike is very _____, but Carl's is really _____. I can carry his bike with one hand.
7 I only have a double bed and a small cupboard in my bedroom. The room's _____ and the bed's _____, so I have no space.

◀ Go back to page 50

145

VOCABULARY PRACTICE

6C Places in a city

1 ▶ 6.15 Match the places in the box with the pictures 1–15. Listen and check.

| apartment block   bridge   cathedral   church   concert hall   library   market |
| monument   mosque   office block   park   skyscraper   square   stadium   theatre |

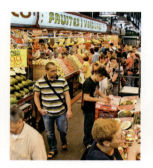
1 _____

2 _____

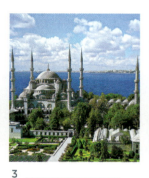
3 _____

4 _____

5 _____

6 _____

7 _____

8 _____

9 _____

10 _____

11 _____

12 _____

13 _____

14 _____

15 _____

2 Match the places in a city with the definitions. Some places go with more than one definition.
1 People live here. _____
2 You go here for entertainment. _____, _____, _____
3 This is a religious building. _____, _____, _____
4 This is usually a tall building. _____, _____, _____
5 This can be outdoors or indoors. _____
6 It is very quiet in this building. _____
7 You often find this in the centre of a square. _____
8 You can sometimes find bars and restaurants here. _____

3 Complete the sentences with places in a city.
1 This famous _____ is for Abraham Lincoln.
2 Let's go to the _____ and buy some food for a picnic.
3 We live on the 9th floor of this _____.
4 You can see the _____ from about 20 kms away. It's very tall.
5 I work in a small _____ in the town centre. It has 4 floors.
6 At the _____, you leave your shoes at the door before you go in.
7 There are concerts and football matches at this _____.
8 You can walk or cycle over this _____, but you can't drive over it.
9 There are concerts in our city's _____ every winter.
10 The central _____ in Wroclaw is really beautiful. There are colourful houses on all four sides.
11 I often go to the _____ to study.

◀ Go back to page 53

COMMUNICATION PRACTICE

1A Student A

1 You are Max. Listen and answer Student B's questions.

Name: Max Lundberg
Nationality: Swedish
Age: 41

2 This is Student B. Ask questions and complete the information.

What's your name? How do you spell it?
_____

Where are you from? _____

How old are you? _____

1C Student A

Look at the people and the possessions. Take turns to ask and answer questions with Student B.
Find out who the following possessions belong to. You can only answer *Yes* or *No*.

Is it Eliza's pen? Are they the children's sweets?

Sarah

the students

the children

Eliza

the Johnsons

Tom

Sadiq

the teacher

1D Student A

1 Look at the contacts. Ask Student B for the missing phone numbers and email addresses. Ask for clarification if you don't understand.

   A *What's Emi's mobile number?*

2 Now listen and answer Student B's questions about the contacts.

Contact	Emi
Mobile	
Email	eesponisa_92@mymail.com
Contact	Geoff
Mobile	0044773493352
Email	
Contact	Liz
Mobile	
Email	liz.sharp87@mymail.com
Contact	Ravi
Mobile	0155584744
Email	

158

COMMUNICATION PRACTICE

2A Student A

1 Listen to Student B and complete the descriptions.

Mark is a ¹_____. He ²_____ in a ³_____. He's from ⁴_____, but he ⁵_____ in Toronto. He ⁶_____ in the evening and he ⁷_____ at the weekend.

Paula is a ⁸_____. She ⁹_____. She's from ¹⁰_____, but she ¹¹_____ in Manchester. She ¹²_____ in the evening, but she ¹³_____ at the weekend.

2 Now describe these people to your partner.

MAYER
Job: mechanic / repairs cars
Place of work: garage
From: Warsaw
Lives: Berlin
Works: evening ✗ weekend ✓

VIVIANA
Job: teacher / teaches English
Place of work: primary school
From: Lisbon
Lives: Rio de Janeiro
Works: evening ✗ weekend ✗

2C Student A

1 You want a flatmate who has a job, likes music and cooks. Student B's friend, Jon, needs a room. Ask Student B questions. Is Jon a good flatmate for you?

 1 where / he / live?
 2 what / he / do?
 3 what / he / do / free time?
 4 he / cook?
 5 he / like / music?

2 Student B wants a flatmate. Your friend, Helen, needs a room. Answer Student B's questions about Helen.

Helen lives with her mother. She works in an office. After work, she goes to the the gym. She doesn't stay in every night – she goes out a lot with her friends. She doesn't like cats.

bad   OK   good

3A Student A

1 How often does Flora do these things? Ask Student B.

 A *How often does Flora go to the cinema?*
 B *She goes to the cinema three times a month.*

2 Answer Student B's questions about Justin.

		Flora	Justin
1	go to the cinema		never
2	cook in the evening		four times a week
3	play online games		every day
4	see his/her grandparents		often
5	go for a run		twice a week
6	listen to the radio		sometimes

3C Student A

Sophia and Sam are a couple. Ask Student B questions about Sam, and answer Student B's questions about Sophia. Find the following:

One thing that Sophia and Sam both love _____
One thing that Sophia and Sam both like _____
One thing that Sophia and Sam both hate _____

 A *Does Sam like art?*   B *No. He hates it!*

Sophia

love ☺☺	like ☺	hate ☹☹
art	cook	jazz
walk the dog	football	go shopping
have a takeaway	go out for dinner	watch TV
do yoga	read magazines	visit family

3D Student A

You want to meet Student B for a coffee this weekend. You're free at the following times. Ask and answer questions to find a time when you're both free.

 A *Would you like to go for a coffee at 10 o'clock on Saturday morning?*
 B *I'm sorry, I can't.*

SATURDAY
Free time
10.00 a.m. – 11.30 a.m.
2.30 p.m. – 3.00 p.m.
6.30 p.m. – 8.30 p.m.
10.00 p.m. – 11.00 p.m.

SUNDAY
Free time
11.00 a.m. – 3.00 p.m.
4.45 p.m. – 6.00 p.m.

COMMUNICATION PRACTICE

4A Student A

1 Look at the pictures of Zak. Ask Student B questions about the missing information. Write the missing times or time expressions. Answer Student B's questions.

   A *When does Zak wake up?*
   B *He wakes up at ...*

1 _____

2 8:15

3 _____

4 midday

5 _____

6 midnight

7 _____

8 Friday nights

9 _____

10 weekend

11 _____

12 winter

2 Compare with Student B. Do you have the same times?

4C Student A

Take turns to describe your picture to Student B and listen to Student B's description. Find six differences between your picture and Student B's picture. Say what the people are doing.

   A *In my picture, Clare and John are having a meal.*
   B *In my picture, they aren't having a meal. They're ...*

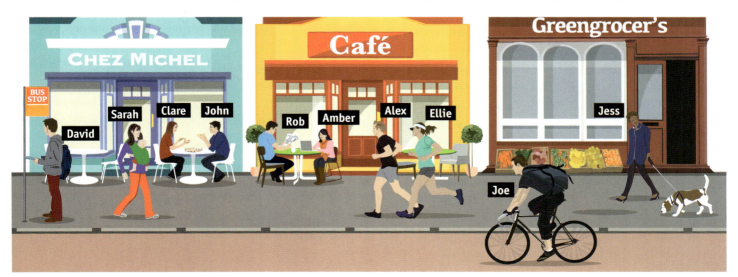

160

COMMUNICATION PRACTICE

5A Student A

1 Look at the pictures. Describe Eric to Student B. Use the words in the boxes to help you.

| have   wear   go to work | | by bike   toast   by bus   jeans and a shirt   a suit   eggs |

Eric usually ...   But today, he ...

2 Listen to Student B's description. Complete the sentences about Emily.
  1 Emily usually has _____ for breakfast, but today she's having _____.
  2 She usually wears _____, but today she's wearing _____.
  3 She usually goes to work _____, but today she's going _____.

3 Check your pictures and sentences with Student B. Do the sentences describe the pictures correctly?

5C Student A

Ask Student B about Alisha and complete the table. Answer Student B's questions about Artur.

A *Can Alisha speak a foreign language?*
B *Yes, she can. She can speak Italian.*

Can he/she ...	Artur	Alisha
... speak a foreign language?	Yes (English and German)	
... dance?	No	
... play a musical instrument?	No	
... ride a horse?	No	
... take good photos?	Yes	
... cook?	Yes (Polish food)	
... repair things?	Yes (bikes)	

5D Student A

1 You are a customer in a department store. Student B is a shop assistant. Student B begins the conversation. Ask him/her these questions.

- Yes, please. Do you sell coats?
- How much is it?
- Do you have this coat in grey?
- Can I try it on?
- Can I pay with this credit card?
- Great. Thanks.

2 You are a shop assistant in a department store. Student B is a customer. Begin the conversation with him/her. Use these sentences.

- Do you need any help?
- Yes, we do. Here are some in a 28.
- We have them in black, blue, green and grey.
- Yes, of course.
- They're near the shoes. I'll show you.
- I'm not sure. Let me ask my colleague. One moment. ... They're 40 pounds.

161

COMMUNICATION PRACTICE

6A Student A

1 Look at the picture and the objects in the box. Ask Student B questions to find out where they are.

| mirror   pictures   books   ball |

A *Is there a mirror above the bed?*   B *No, there isn't.*

2 Answer Student B's questions about his/her missing objects. You can only answer *yes* or *no*.

6C Student A

1 A Look at the information about three cities. Ask Student B for the missing information and write it in the chart.

A *Is the market square in Blue City busy?*   B *Yes. It's very busy.*

B Answer Student B's questions.

Blue City	Yellowtown	Greenville
mosque – really beautiful ✔	beach – clean?	Old Town – quite pretty ✔
market square – busy?	restaurants – not very expensive ✘	cathedral – beautiful?
museum – really interesting ✔	local people – friendly?	Central Park – not very clean ✘
art gallery – good?	hotels – really nice ✔	river – clean?
food and drink – not expensive at all ✘	museum – interesting?	monuments – not very famous ✘

2 Decide which city you want to visit in pairs.

A *I want to go to Yellowtown because it has really nice hotels.*   B *Yes, but the beach isn't very clean.*

162

COMMUNICATION PRACTICE

1A Student B

1 This is Student A. Ask questions and complete the information.

What's your name? How do you spell it?
_____

Where are you from? _____

How old are you? _____

2 You are Li. Listen and answer Student A's questions.

Name: Li Yang
Nationality: Chinese
Age: 24

1C Student B

Look at the people and the possessions. Take turns to ask and answer questions with Student A.
Find out who the following possessions belong to. You can only answer *Yes* or *No*.

Is it Tom's phone?   Is it the Johnsons' umbrella?

Sarah

the students

the children

Eliza

the Johnsons

Tom

Sadiq

the teacher

1D Student B

1 Look at the contacts. Listen and answer Student A's questions.

2 Now ask Student A for the missing phone numbers and email addresses. Ask for clarification if you don't understand.

B *What's Emi's email address?*

Contact	Emi
Mobile	003466606326
Email	

Contact	Geoff
Mobile	
Email	jones_geoffrey@hotmail.co.uk

Contact	Liz
Mobile	00775003199
Email	

Contact	Ravi
Mobile	
Email	r.d.g.freelance@yahoo.com

COMMUNICATION PRACTICE

2A Student B

1 Describe these people to your partner.

MARK
Job: nurse / in a hospital
From: Chicago
Lives: Toronto
Works: evening ✓ weekend ✓

PAULA
Job: chef / cooks Japanese food
From: Sydney
Lives: Manchester
Works: evening ✗ weekend ✓

2 Now listen to Student A and complete the descriptions.

Mayer is a [1]_____. He [2]_____ in a [3]_____. He's from [4]_____, but he [5]_____ in Berlin. He [6]_____ in the evening, but he [7]_____ at the weekend.

Viviana is a [8]_____. She [9]_____ in a [10]_____. She's from [11]_____, but she [12]_____ in Rio de Janeiro. She [13]_____ in the evening and she [14]_____ at the weekend.

2C Student B

1 Student A wants a flatmate. Your friend, Jon, needs a room. Answer Student A's questions about Jon.

> Jon lives with his parents. He's a student. In his free time, he plays the guitar. He doesn't cook. He has a girlfriend. He loves music.

2 You want a flatmate who has a job, doesn't stay in every night and likes cats (you have one). Student A's friend, Helen, needs a room. Ask Student A questions. Is Helen a good flatmate for you?

1 where / she / live ?
2 what / she / do ?
3 what / she / do / after work ?
4 she / stay in / every night ?
5 she / like / cats ?

bad   OK   good

3A Student B

1 Answer Student A's questions about Flora.

A *How often does Flora go to the cinema?*
B *She goes to the cinema three times a month.*

2 How often does Justin do these things? Ask Student A.

		Flora	Justin
1	go to the cinema	three times a month	
2	cook in the evening	rarely	
3	play online games	never	
4	see his/her grandparents	every day	
5	go for a run	once a week	
6	listen to the radio	often	

3C Student B

Sophia and Sam are a couple. Ask Student A questions about Sophia, and answer Student A's questions about Sam. Find the following:

One thing that Sophia and Sam both love _____
One thing that Sophia and Sam both like _____
One thing that Sophia and Sam both hate _____

B *Does Sophia like having a takeaway?*
A *Yes. She loves it!*

Sam

love ☺☺	like ☺	hate ☹
jazz	football	cook
go out for dinner	have a takeaway	go shopping
walk the dog	watch TV	art
visit family	do yoga	read magazines

3D Student B

You want to meet Student A to go for a run this weekend. You're free at the following times. Ask and answer questions to find a time when you're both free.

B *Would you like to go for a run at 8.45 on Saturday morning?*
A *I'm sorry, I can't.*

SATURDAY
Free time
8.30 a.m. – 10.00 a.m
1.30 p.m – 2.30 p.m
5.30 p.m – 6.30 p.m

SUNDAY
Free time
12.00 p.m – 4.00 p.m
7.30 p.m – 9.30 p.m

COMMUNICATION PRACTICE

4A Student B

1 Look at the pictures of Zak. Ask Student A questions about the missing information. Write the missing times or time expressions. Answer Student A's questions.

   B *When does Zak walk the dog?*
   A *He walks the dog at ...*

1 7:25

2 _____

3 9:00 – 5:30

4 _____

5 22:00 – 23:45

6 _____

7 Wednesday evenings

8 _____

9 Saturday mornings

10 _____

11 summer

12 _____

2 Compare with Student A. Do you have the same times?

4C Student B

1 Take turns to describe your picture to Student A and listen to Student A's description. Find six differences between your picture and Student A's picture. Say what the people re doing.

   A *In my picture, Clare and John are having a meal.*
   B *In my picture, they aren't having a meal. They're ...*

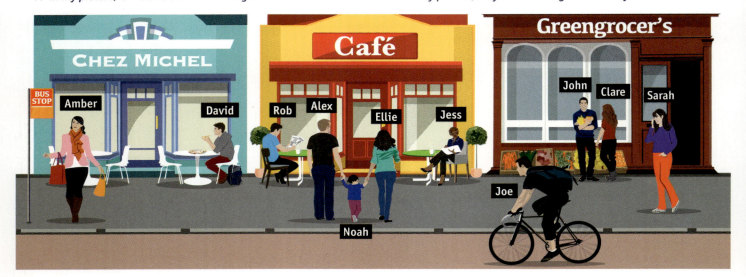

169

COMMUNICATION PRACTICE

5A Student B

1 Listen to Student A's description. Complete the sentences about Eric.
  1 Eric usually has _____ for breakfast, but today he's having _____.
  2 He usually wears _____, but today he's wearing _____.
  3 He usually goes to work _____, but today he's going _____.

2 Look at the pictures. Describe Emily to Student A. Use the words in the boxes to help you.

| have   wear   go to work | trousers and a jumper   coffee   a skirt and a top   on the underground   by car   tea |

Emily usually ...   But today, she ...

3 Check your pictures and sentences with Student A. Do the sentences describe the pictures correctly?

5C Student B

1 Ask Student A about Artur and complete the table. Answer Student A's questions about Alisha.

  B *Can Artur play a musical instrument?*
  A *No, he can't.*

Can he/she ...	Artur	Alisha
... speak a foreign language?		Yes (Italian)
... dance?		Yes (the Tango)
... play a musical instrument?		Yes (the drums)
... ride a horse?		No
... take good photos?		No
... cook?		Yes (Italian food)
... repair things?		Yes (computers)

5D Student B

1 You are a shop assistant in a department store. Student A is a customer. Begin the conversation with him/her. Use these sentences.

- Yes, we do. I'll show you where they are.
- It's 60 pounds.
- Just a moment, I'll check. Yes. Here you are.
- Yes, we take all credit cards.
- Yes, of course. The changing rooms are over there.
- Hello. Can I help you?

2 You are a customer in a department store. Student A is a shop assistant. Student A begins the conversation. Ask him/her these questions.

- And what colours are there?
- Lovely. Thanks.
- Yes, please. Do you have these trousers in a size 28?
- Thanks. Can I try them on?
- Thanks. How much are they?
- Where are the changing rooms?

170

COMMUNICATION PRACTICE

6A Student B

1 Look at the picture and answer Student A's questions about his/her missing objects. You can only answer *yes* or *no*.

A **Is there a mirror above the bed?**   B **No, there isn't.**

2 Look at the objects in the box. Ask Student A questions to find out where they are.

| shoes   clock   shelves   lamp |

6C Student B

1 A Look at the information about three cities. Answer Student A's questions..

B Ask Student A for the missing information and write it in the chart.

B **Is the mosque in Blue City beautiful?**   A **Yes. It's really beautiful.**

Blue City	Yellowtown	Greenville
mosque – beautiful?	beach – not very clean ✘	Old Town – pretty?
market square – very busy ✔	restaurants – expensive?	cathedral – really beautiful ✔
museum – interesting?	local people – really friendly ✔	Central Park – clean?
art gallery – not very good ✘	hotels – nice?	river – quite clean ✔
food and drink – expensive?	museum – not interesting at all ✘	monuments – famous?

2 Decide which city you want to visit in pairs.

A **I want to go to Yellowtown because it has really nice hotels.**   B **Yes, but the beach isn't very clean.**

IRREGULAR VERBS

Infinitive	Past simple	Past participle
be	was, were	been
become	became	become
begin	began	begun
bite	bit	bitten
break	broke	broken
bring	brought	brought
build	built	built
buy	bought	bought
choose	chose	chosen
come	came	come
cost	cost	cost
do	did	done
dream	dreamt/dreamed	dreamt/dreamed
forbid	forbade	forbidden
forget	forgot	forgotten
forgive	forgave	forgiven
get	got	got
give	gave	given
go	went	gone, been
grow	grew	grown
have	had	had
hear	heard	heard
hide	hid	hidden
hold	held	held
keep	kept	kept
know	knew	known
learn	learnt/learned	learnt/learned
leave	left	left
let	let	let
lose	lost	lost

Infinitive	Past simple	Past participle
make	made	made
meet	met	met
pay	paid	paid
put	put	put
read (/riːd/)	read (/red/)	read (/red/)
ride	rode	ridden
ring	rang	rung
rise	rose	risen
run	ran	run
say	said	said
see	saw	seen
sell	sold	sold
send	sent	sent
sleep	slept	slept
speak	spoke	spoken
spend	spent	spent
stand	stood	stood
steal	stole	stolen
stick	stuck	stuck
swim	swam	swum
take	took	taken
teach	taught	taught
tell	told	told
think	thought	thought
throw	threw	thrown
understand	understood	understood
wake	woke	woken
wear	wore	worn
win	won	won
write	wrote	written

Personal Best

Workbook

A2
Elementary

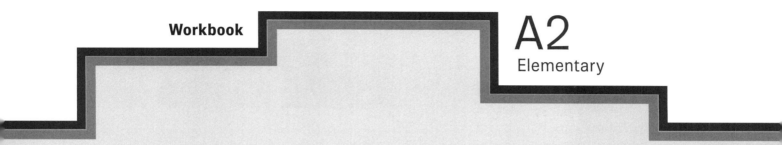

Richmond

UNIT 1

You and me

1A LANGUAGE

GRAMMAR: The verb *be*

1 Choose the correct options to complete the sentences.

1 I *am / is / are* nineteen years old.
2 She *am / is / are* a teacher.
3 *Am / Is / Are* you from this country?
4 They *am not / isn't / aren't* at home.
5 We *am / is / are* all in the same class.
6 *Am / Is / Are* she English?
7 I *'m not / isn't / aren't* hungry.
8 It *am / is / are* nice to meet you.

2 Complete the sentences with the correct form of the verb *be*.

1 'Where's Malu?' 'I don't know. She _____ here.'
2 'Are you twenty?' 'No, I _____ twenty-two.'
3 My parents _____ in New York this week.
4 'Is Pablo your brother?' 'No. He _____ my friend.'
5 'Where are the children?' 'They _____ at home. They're at school.'
6 '_____ we all here?' 'No, James is in the classroom.'
7 You _____ a teacher. You're a student.
8 '_____ she Russian?' 'No, she's Polish.'

VOCABULARY: Countries and nationalities and numbers 1–1,000

3 Write the words or numbers.

1 95 _____
2 twenty-one _____
3 47 _____
4 two thousand _____
5 12 _____
6 six hundred and thirty _____
7 802 _____
8 eighty-five _____
9 13 _____
10 fifteen _____

4 Match flags a–f with nationalities 1–6.

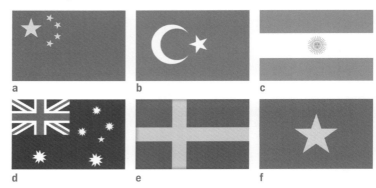

1 Swedish ___
2 Chinese ___
3 Australian ___
4 Argentinian ___
5 Vietnamese ___
6 Turkish ___

5 Complete the sentences with countries or nationalities.

1 My mum's from Japan. She's _____.
2 Our teacher is from _____. She's Canadian.
3 I'm from Ireland. I'm _____.
4 His best friend is from _____. She's Italian.
5 Marta is from Portugal. She's _____.
6 My dad's from the USA. He's _____.
7 They are _____. They're from Wales.
8 We are from Spain. We're _____.
9 Michel's _____. He's from France.
10 Wahid is from Egypt. He's _____.

PRONUNCIATION: Contractions of *be*

6 ▶ 1.1 Underline the contractions. Say the sentences. Listen, check and repeat.

1 'Are you eighteen years old?' 'No, I'm twenty.'
2 'Where is Miguel?' 'He's in a meeting.'
3 This is the café. We're eating breakfast here.
4 Anna is my sister. She's an English teacher.
5 They're my friends. We are in the same class.
6 I know you. You're Sasha's brother.
7 'Is your car German?' 'No, it's Italian.'

SKILLS 1B

READING: Approaching a text

My trip with the orchestra

Hi! I'm Paola and I'm from Portugal. I ¹_____ a student, but I'm also in a guitar orchestra for young people. At the moment, I'm on a trip with the orchestra. We're ready to play concerts in London, Paris and Rome! Here's my blog about my month of music.

WEEK 1

These are some of my friends from the orchestra. They ²_____ great fun! Maria ³_____ nineteen and Miguel is eighteen. They're my best friends. We usually go to the park together – we all like nature. We're in London at the moment, and there are lots of beautiful parks here.

WEEK 2

Our guitar teacher's name is Carlos and he's very friendly. He is a great teacher – and he also cooks dinner for us every night. We all like his food very much.

WEEK 3

We ⁴_____ in Paris now, in a hotel near the city centre. There are a lot of English students in this hotel, so I practise my English every day. The orchestra plays music every morning until midday, and then we walk around the city. It's a really interesting place and we see and do lots of things.

WEEK 4

We're in Rome now. It ⁵_____ an exciting city! Our concerts ⁶_____ in the evening, and we go shopping every day. My month of music is nearly finished. I'm happy because I want to see my family, but I'm sad because this trip is great.

---

1. Look at the title, headings and pictures. Choose the best description for the text.
   a Someone who goes to music school every day.
   b Someone who travels with her orchestra for four weeks.
   c Someone who visits Rome in the holidays.

2. Complete the text with the correct forms of the verb *be*.

3. Are the sentences true (T), false (F) or doesn't say (DS)?
   1 Paola is Portuguese. _____
   2 Her friend Maria is Spanish. _____
   3 There are nice parks in London. _____
   4 Carlos is a bad cook. _____
   5 There are no French students in the hotel in Paris. _____
   6 Miguel doesn't like Paris. _____
   7 Paola likes Rome. _____
   8 Maria and Miguel like shopping in Rome. _____

3

1C LANGUAGE

GRAMMAR: Possessive adjectives and 's for possession

1 Choose the correct options to complete the sentences.

1 My classmates and I all like ____ English teacher.
   a our   b his   c their
2 'What is your ____ name?' 'Her name's Giulia.'
   a sisters   b sisters'   c sister's
3 'Is this ____ key?' 'Yes – it's mine.'
   a my   b your   c her
4 Do you like ____ shoes? They're new!
   a Jame's   b James   c James'
5 'Where does Enrico live?' '____ house is over there.'
   a Its   b His   c Your
6 'Is Emma at home?' 'No. Her ____ car isn't here.'
   a parents   b parent's   c parents'
7 I have a white cat. ____ name is Snowy.
   a My   b Their   c Its
8 This shop doesn't have ____ bags.
   a womens   b women's   c womens'

2 Complete the text with possessive adjectives.

I'm Juan and this is a photo of ¹____ class. You can see my best friend – ²____ name's Marta – and ³____ teacher. ⁴____ name is Pedro and he has two children. ⁵____ names are Luisa and Carlos.

This is a photo of my house. Mum and I live here. It's a small house, but ⁶____ garden is quite big – we both like gardening! We have a cat, too – ⁷____ name is Sooty because it is black and white. What about you? What are ⁸____ friends and house like?

VOCABULARY: Personal objects

3 Match definitions 1–6 with objects a–f.

1 You can see your face in this. ____
2 You open a door with this. ____
3 You can talk to your friends with it. ____
4 You wear these on your hands when it's cold. ____
5 You need this when it rains. ____
6 You put your money in it. ____

   a umbrella
   b purse
   c phone
   d gloves
   e key
   f mirror

4 Complete the words.

1 This is a p ___ ___ ___ ___ of me with my mum and my sister. We are on holiday!
2 You can buy a s ___ ___ ___ ___ for your postcard at the post office.
3 What's the time? I don't have a w ___ ___ ___ ___.
4 When I walk at night, I take a t ___ ___ ___ ___ to help me see.
5 My name and address are on my i ___ ___ ___ ___ ___ ___ ___ c ___ ___ ___.
6 I eat a lot of s ___ ___ ___ ___ ___. My mum says they're bad for my teeth.
7 I can't read this without my g ___ ___ ___ ___ ___.
8 We can't eat c ___ ___ ___ ___ ___ ___ g ___ ___ ___ in lessons.

PRONUNCIATION: Sentence stress

5 ▶1.2 Listen and repeat the sentences. Underline the stressed words in each sentence. Listen again, check and repeat.

1 What's in his wallet?
2 Here are your books.
3 My tablet is on the chair.
4 What's her name?
5 Their house is new.
6 Where are my tissues?

SKILLS 1D

SPEAKING: Asking for and giving personal information

1 ▶1.3 Listen to the conversation. Which sentence is correct?

 A Miguel is at home.
 B Miguel is on the phone.
 C Miguel is at the gym.

2 ▶1.3 Listen again. Complete the sentences.

 1 What's your f_____ name?
 2 And what's your _____?
 3 Do you have an _____ address, Miguel?
 4 And what's your _____ number, please?
 5 What's your a_____?
 6 OK. What's your p_____?

3 ▶1.3 Listen again and complete the form below.

4 ▶1.3 Does the receptionist ask for clarification for Miguel's information? Listen again and write A, B or C for 1–6.

 A Yes, she asks 'How do you spell that (please)?'
 B Yes, she asks Miguel to repeat information.
 C No, she doesn't ask for clarification.

 1 first name ____
 2 surname ____
 3 email address ____
 4 phone number ____
 5 address ____
 6 postcode ____

5 ▶1.4 Look at the information in the form below. Listen and check if it is correct. Ask for clarification and make sure you use polite intonation.

SUPERFIT GYM — Date:

CLIENT INFORMATION
First name:
Surname:

CONTACT DETAILS
Email: _____@starmail.com
Phone number: 077
Address: 30 _____ Road
Postcode:

SUPERFIT GYM — Date:

CLIENT INFORMATION
First name: MARIA
Surname: PALMA

CONTACT DETAILS
Email: palma90@newmail.co.uk
Phone number: 07700990816
Address: 13 Broughton Road
Postcode: EH5 7AZ

1 REVIEW and PRACTICE

LISTENING

1 ▶ 1.5 Listen to the podcast about an interesting street. Read the sentences. Are they true (T) or false (F)?

1 Narborough Road is in the UK. _____
2 It's interesting because it's a very international street. _____
3 Jacob's shop sells stamps. _____
4 His mother is from Wales. _____
5 Mr Deng is Japanese. _____
6 He cooks and serves food. _____
7 Maria is Portuguese. _____
8 Anna is from Australia. _____

2 ▶ 1.5 Listen again. Complete the sentences with the numbers in the box. There are three numbers you don't need.

| 2 | 3 | 4 | 23 | 73 |
| 118 | 122 | 180 | 222 | |

1 Jacob's shop sells _____ different types of sweets.
2 There are about _____ shops on Narborough Road.
3 People from _____ different countries have shops there.
4 Mr Deng has _____ restaurants.
5 Maria has _____ children.
6 Anna has _____ sisters.

READING

1 Read the blog on page 7 about an international home. Write the people's nationalities.

1 Suki _____
2 Lucja _____
3 Ryan _____
4 Simona _____
5 Marco _____

2 Circle the countries in the blog and underline the personal objects.

3 Are the sentences true (T), false (F) or doesn't say (DS)?

1 Suki is from France. _____
2 Five people live in Suki's flat. _____
3 Lucja speaks English well. _____
4 Suki is eighteen years old. _____
5 Ryan is a student. _____
6 Ryan works in a shop in Paris. _____
7 Simona doesn't like the weather in Brazil. _____
8 Simona's family live in Brazil. _____
9 Marco has a job in Paris. _____
10 Marco is Suki's boyfriend. _____

REVIEW and PRACTICE 1

HOME   BLOG   PODCASTS   ABOUT   CONTACT

Guest blogger Penny writes about people living in another country.

AN INTERNATIONAL HOME

All around the world, young people live and study away from their own homes. But what's it like living with people from other countries? I asked Suki, a photography student. Suki's from Vietnam, but she lives in France at the moment. Here's what she says about life in her international home.

> I live in a flat in Paris with four other people. We're all from different countries, but we can all speak English really well. Our flat is very friendly and of course it has a great international atmosphere!

Lucja is from Poland and she's eighteen years old. She is a student, like me. She wants to be a dentist, but she really loves sweets! Lucja's a very happy person – I like her a lot. Here's a photo of her looking happy.

Ryan is twenty-five years old and he is from Ireland. He works in a café near our flat. He likes shopping and he loves shopping for clothes. Here's a photo of him wearing his favourite sunglasses. He thinks they are very cool!

Simona is from Brazil. She's twenty-one years old and she's a nurse. She doesn't like the weather here – she is always cold! I think she is unhappy because she can't see her family back home very often and she misses the sun. Here's Simona with her favourite umbrella – she takes it everywhere she goes!

Marco is from Italy. He's a student, too, but he wants to be a model. He's very handsome, isn't he? He's 23 years old and he likes cars, football and looking in the mirror!

Who do you live with? Tell us about them and where you live. Don't forget to send us some photographs, too!

7

UNIT 2

Work and play

2A LANGUAGE

GRAMMAR: Present simple: positive and negative

1 Choose the correct options to complete the sentences.

1 He _____ a taxi every evening.
  a drives   b drive
  c don't drive

2 My sister _____ English – she teaches Maths.
  a teach   b doesn't teach
  c teaches

3 I like my job, but it _____ very well.
  a doesn't pay   b pays
  c pay

4 At the weekend, I'm a tour guide. I _____ tourists around my city.
  a doesn't take   b takes
  c take

5 I speak French, but I _____ German.
  a don't speak   b speaks
  c speak

6 My mum _____ in a restaurant. She serves food.
  a work   b works
  c don't work

2 Complete the email with the correct present simple form of the verbs in brackets.

Hi Malin,

How are you? I am very busy at the moment.
I ¹_____ (work) a lot of hours every day.

We ²_____ (have) a new teacher at school – Mrs Black. She ³_____ (teach) us English and French. She's very funny – everyone ⁴_____ (like) her. Mrs Black loves films, and we ⁵_____ (watch) a lot of interesting videos in her class. She ⁶_____ (live) here, though – she drives from London every day!

Mum and dad say 'hello'! They are busy, too. The restaurant is very popular and they ⁷_____ (serve) food and drink all day, every day!

Write soon,

Tamara

VOCABULARY: Jobs and job verbs

3 Order the letters to make words for jobs.

1 My mum's a TRODCO. She works in a hospital.
  _____

2 I'm a student, but on Friday nights I'm a GISREN with my band.
  _____

3 Ask a CAIMNECH to look at your car.
  _____

4 You must be good at Maths to work as an TONCANACUT.
  _____

5 I love travelling, so I want to be a THIGLF NETTANDTA.
  _____

6 I need to go to the STINTED. My teeth hurt.
  _____

7 My sister works as a TOESCIRENPIT in a hotel.
  _____

8 This light is broken. I must call an CAINCLEETRI.
  _____

4 Complete the sentences with job verbs.

1 Julio is a waiter. He _____ food in a restaurant.
2 My hairdresser _____ my hair every month.
3 Her aunt is a shop assistant. She _____ computers in a big shop.
4 He always _____ a suit to work because he's a lawyer.
5 Sonia is a tour guide. She _____ tourists with their questions.
6 His brother is a famous chef. He _____ food in the best hotel in Rome.

PRONUNCIATION: -s and -es endings

5 ▶ 2.1 Listen and circle the sound that you hear at the end of the underlined verb. Listen again, check and repeat.

1 Suki <u>works</u> in a restaurant.	/s/	/z/	/ɪz/
2 Anna <u>watches</u> TV every day.	/s/	/z/	/ɪz/
3 Sally <u>helps</u> her brother with his homework.	/s/	/z/	/ɪz/
4 Jean Paul <u>drives</u> an Italian car.	/s/	/z/	/ɪz/
5 Ester really <u>likes</u> chocolate.	/s/	/z/	/ɪz/
6 Roberto <u>lives</u> in Argentina.	/s/	/z/	/ɪz/
7 Max <u>teaches</u> Science.	/s/	/z/	/ɪz/
8 Turgay <u>sells</u> shoes.	/s/	/z/	/ɪz/

SKILLS 2B

LISTENING: Listening for names, places, days and times

1 ▶ 2.2 Listen to the conversation between two friends. Which names and places do you hear?

1	a	Janine	b	Jenny	c	Joan
2	a	Donna	b	Donald	c	Danny
3	a	Mateo's	b	Maria's	c	Marco's
4	a	Oxford	b	Dartford	c	Stratford
5	a	Vicky	b	Vinny	c	Ricky

2 ▶ 2.2 Complete the sentences with *in*, *on* or *at*. Then listen again and check.

1 Vanessa plays tennis ____ seven o'clock.
2 She eats pizza ____ the Italian restaurant.
3 ____ Thursday night, she studies.
4 She is always ____ Oxford on Friday evenings.
5 Paul watches TV ____ Saturday evening.
6 Paul's favourite TV show starts ____ eight o'clock.

3 Match the words to make activities.

1	play	____	a	friends
2	read	____	b	to music
3	meet	____	c	the guitar
4	spend time	____	d	English
5	go out	____	e	a film
6	see	____	f	with my family
7	study	____	g	for dinner
8	listen	____	h	the newspaper

4 Complete the sentences with six of the activities from exercise 3. Use the correct form of the verbs. Use positives and negatives.

1 She's the singer in the band and she also _____.
2 I _____ at home. I normally watch TV.
3 They _____ every day. They know a lot about the world.
4 She _____ at the new language academy in the city centre.
5 We _____ every week. We really like Italian restaurants.
6 Now that I am at university, I _____ except for the holidays.

5 ▶ 2.3 Read the sentences. Underline the words that only have the sound /ə/. Then listen and check.

1 Do you like music?
2 My sister's a teacher.
3 I want to play tennis!
4 What do you do in your free time?
5 He goes to school on Saturday morning.
6 Where is the cinema?

9

2C LANGUAGE

GRAMMAR: Present simple: questions

1 Complete the sentences with the words in the box.

| what | do | who | does (x 2) | how |
| when | where | don't (x 2) | | |

1 _____ you play football?
2 'Does she work here?' 'Yes, she _____.'
3 _____ do you go after work?
4 'Do they like dogs?' 'No, they _____.'
5 _____ does he live with?
6 _____ does the lesson start?
7 _____ your father speak Italian?
8 'Do you know Lisa?' 'No, we _____.'
9 _____ do they do at the weekend?
10 _____ do you say this word?

2 Order the words to make questions.

1 does / learn / where / he / Turkish
   _____?
2 Vietnam / you / come from / do
   _____?
3 she / a cat / does / have
   _____?
4 with / they / who / do / go out
   _____?
5 at / do / start work / eight / we
   _____?
6 you / do / why / to school / drive
   _____?
7 does / repair / where / she / cars
   _____?
8 suit / wear / he / a / does
   _____?

PRONUNCIATION: Auxiliary do/does in questions

3 Look at the pictures. Use the prompts to write questions about Carla.

1 where/live?
   _____
2 how/work?
   _____
3 when/home?
   _____
4 do/study/evening?
   _____
5 what/weekends?
   _____
6 who/cinema?
   _____

4 ▶ 2.4 Say the questions. How do we say *do* and *does*? Listen, check and repeat.

1 Do you like pizza?
2 Does he live with his parents?
3 What do you do at the weekend?
4 Do they speak Spanish?
5 Where does he work?
6 When do you watch TV?
7 Does your sister teach yoga?
8 Who do you spend time with in the evening?

SKILLS 2D

WRITING: Opening and closing an informal email

Hey Lucy,

How are things with you? Do you like your new home in London?

Here in Madrid everything is fine. I have a new flatmate. She is really nice and friendly, but I often think of you and wish you were here! Her name is Keira and she's from New Zealand. She's a good cook, but she doesn't make great chocolate cake like you!

I have a new part-time job. I'm a tour guide – I take people around Madrid and show them the sights. I work every afternoon, from 2 p.m. till 6 or 7 p.m. I really like my job, but I don't have a lot of free time at the moment! You can see me working in this photo.

In the evenings, I am quite tired, but I sometimes play tennis with Keira. At the weekends, I usually go to the cinema or go shopping.

Take care,
Maria

1 Read Maria's email then look at the phrases below. Are they opening (O) or closing (C) phrases?

1 Hi ____
2 Write soon with your news! ____
3 See you soon ____
4 Hello ____
5 Hi Marta ____
6 Love Freddie XXX ____

2 Find and underline the connectors in the email.

3 Choose the correct connectors.

1 I really like coffee *and* / *but* I don't like tea at all.
2 Is that your mother *and* / *or* is it your sister?
3 I go to school *and* / *so* I also have extra English lessons.
4 I'm from Spain, *but* / *and* I now live in Mexico.
5 I have two sisters: Vanessa *and* / *or* Sally.
6 Are you a teacher *or* / *but* a student?

4 Complete the email with *and*, *but* or *or*.

Hi Samantha,

I'm on holiday in Granada in Spain. Our holiday is really fun ¹_____ exciting ²_____ I wish you were here. I think it's the perfect place for you. You can choose to go to the beach ³_____ the mountains. The food ⁴_____ drink is lovely ⁵_____ people have lunch too late! They don't eat until 3 o'clock!!!

I will call you soon ⁶_____ write another email.

Bye,
Clare

5 Write an email to a friend in another country. Use *and*, *but* and *or* to connect your ideas. Include:

- an informal opening phrase
- information about your home, friends and free time
- an informal closing phrase.

11

2 REVIEW and PRACTICE

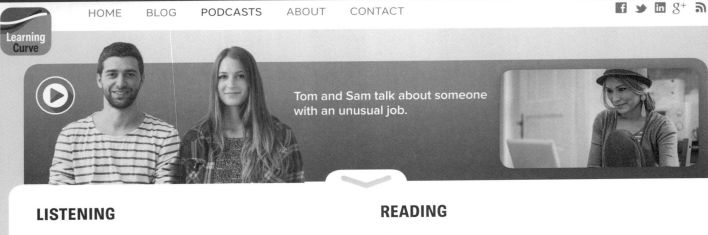

LISTENING

1 ▶ 2.5 Listen to the podcast about someone with an interesting job. Choose the correct answers.

1 Which sentence about Arabella is true?
   a She doesn't like going to the cinema.
   b Her hobby is also her job.
   c She reads a lot of newspapers.

2 What is Arabella's job?
   a She sells tickets at a cinema.
   b She's the manager of a magazine.
   c She writes about films.

3 What does Arabella say about Luke?
   a He really likes films.
   b He is her friend.
   c He doesn't talk a lot.

2 ▶ 2.5 Listen again. Complete the sentences with one or two words.

1 Arabella really loves her _____.
2 She writes about films for _____ and magazines.
3 She goes to the cinema _____ times a week.
4 She really likes horror _____.
5 After she sees a film, she likes to _____ it.
6 She also writes about _____.

3 ▶ 2.5 Order the words to make questions. Listen again and check your answers.

1 go / do / you / every night / to the cinema ?
   _____

2 what kind / like / you / do / of films ?
   _____

3 you / take / with you / a friend / do ?
   _____

4 have / you / do / another job ?
   _____

READING

1 Read the blog on page 13 about work and free time. Answer the questions.

1 What is Tom Fletcher's job?
2 Does Tom think we have a good work-life balance?
3 What does Tom think we need to spend more time doing?

2 Does Tom say the things below? Choose Yes or No.

1	Many people start work at seven o'clock.	Yes	No
2	People work more hours in winter.	Yes	No
3	Tom has his lunch at home.	Yes	No
4	Many people always feel tired.	Yes	No
5	Playing the guitar can make you feel good.	Yes	No
6	Meeting friends is a good idea.	Yes	No
7	We must all walk for fifteen minutes every day.	Yes	No
8	More free time is also good for your family.	Yes	No

3 Circle the free-time activities in the blog.

REVIEW and PRACTICE 2

HOME BLOG PODCASTS ABOUT CONTACT

 Guest blogger Kate writes about ideas for a work–life balance.

Work or life?

Today, lots of people work or study for more than 50 hours a week. We don't have much free time in the week. But it's important to have a 'work–life balance' and to have some time away from work and studying. What can we do to make sure we don't work too much? Here are some ideas from life coach, Tom Fletcher.

People work really hard these days. Think about it – most of us read our work emails before breakfast! Then we work until seven o'clock. In winter, we probably don't see the sun! 60% of us take work home, too – and check our work emails late at night.

This is what a lot of people tell me about their day: 'I get up at six o'clock, eat lunch at my desk and go home at ten o'clock at night. I don't have time to go to a restaurant or to meet friends. I don't spend time with my family either – I'm always too busy. I want to relax, but there isn't enough time in the day. I'm always tired and I don't really enjoy my life at the moment.'

This isn't good for our minds or bodies. You need to make time for life, because it's important to do things that you enjoy. Listen to music, play the guitar, read a book or go to the cinema – these are things that make you feel good. And when you feel good, you can also work better.

Free-time activities don't need a lot of time – it's easy to make small changes to your day. Do you eat your lunch at your desk? Why not go out to a café – it's much more fun! Try to meet friends every day. Go for a fifteen-minute walk together. It makes you feel great and gives you more energy!

UNIT 3

People in my life

3A LANGUAGE

GRAMMAR: Adverbs and expressions of frequency

1 Order the words to make sentences.

1 always / is / your sister / late for school
   _____.

2 together / eats dinner / our family / once a week
   _____.

3 grandparents / sees / his / he / twice a month
   _____.

4 because / play tennis / I / never / I don't like it
   _____.

5 breakfast / they / eat / sometimes / a big
   _____.

6 in the kitchen / a day / helps my mother / my brother / three times
   _____.

2 Complete the conversation with adverbs and expressions of frequency.

Anas What do you [1]u_____ do in the summer holidays?

Sara I travel to the USA [2]o_____ a year.

Anas Lucky you!

Sara Well, my family live there and I don't [3]o_____ see them. But I visit my cousins [4]t_____ a month because they live near me. What about you?

Anas I stay at home [5]e_____ year.

Sara Really? Isn't that boring?

Anas Not at all! I work in a café three [6]t_____ a week and I see my friends every day.

VOCABULARY: Family

3 Match the two parts of the sentences.

1 My aunt ____
2 My mother-in-law ____
3 My nephew ____
4 My grandparents ____
5 My niece ____
6 My sister-in-law ____

a is my husband's sister.
b is my brother's son.
c is my mother's sister.
d is my wife's mother.
e are my parents' mother and father.
f is my sister's daughter.

4 Complete the family words.

This is a photo of my family. This is me. I have one [1]s_____. Her name's Sal and this is her [2]h_____, Ali. He's also my [3]b_____-i_____-l_____, of course! They have two [4]c_____ – both boys, called Casper and John – who are my [5]n_____. My [6]f_____ took the photo. His brother Fred is my favourite [7]u_____!

PRONUNCIATION: Sentence stress

5 ▶ 3.1 Read the sentences. Stress the adverbs and expressions of frequency. Listen, check and repeat.

1 He sometimes visits his cousin.
2 We're never late.
3 I study English every day.
4 I see my nephew once a week.
5 We often eat Chinese food.
6 I usually go to the park with my niece.

SKILLS 3B

READING: Scanning a text

HOLIDAYS WITH A DIFFERENCE!

IT'S HOLIDAY TIME! READ ABOUT OUR ACTIVE HOLIDAYS
WHICH ONE DO YOU LIKE BEST?

A PONY TREKKING

Our pony trekking holidays are very popular. On these holidays, you stay in a quiet hotel in a beautiful place. Then you get up early and go pony trekking until 3 p.m. with one of our friendly guides. You also learn all about pony care.

C TAKE A BREAK – WITH A YOGA HOLIDAY

Are you busy at work? Are you always tired? Relax and spend time with other people who love yoga. You stay in a beautiful small house beside the sea. In the morning you practise yoga and go swimming in the sea. In the afternoon and evening you eat our healthy food (it's also delicious!).

B SINGING IN SUMMER!

Do you love music? Then this holiday is for you. On this special holiday you sing in a group every morning for two hours. Then, in the afternoon, you give group concerts in the town centre. In the evening, you relax and sometimes go dancing, too. It's a lot of fun!

D ARTS AND CRAFTS

Our arts and crafts holiday is for people who love to make things. Every morning you learn a different craft and in the afternoon you go on trips to visit different artists. In the evening you show the other students your work. It's a fun holiday and it's interesting, too!

1 Scan the text. On which holiday do you:
1 eat delicious food? _____
2 dance in the evenings? _____
3 stay in a hotel? _____
4 learn different crafts? _____

2 Are the sentences true (T), false (F) or doesn't say (DS)?
1 On the pony trekking holiday, you go riding with a guide. _____
2 You can go swimming in the evening on the pony trekking holiday. _____
3 You meet people from different countries on the singing holiday. _____
4 On the singing holiday, you can relax in the evenings. _____
5 You buy and cook your own food on the yoga holiday. _____
6 On the yoga holiday, you stay near the sea. _____
7 On the arts and crafts holiday, other people can look at your work. _____
8 You make different things in the afternoon on the arts and crafts holiday. _____

3 Complete the sentences with *also* or *too*.
1 These holidays sound good! I like the yoga holiday and the singing holiday, _____.
2 I want to go on the pony trekking holiday and I _____ want to go on the yoga holiday.
3 I like ponies and I _____ like quiet hotels.
4 On the arts and crafts holiday, you make art and you look at other people's work, _____.
5 Singing is fun and it's relaxing, _____.
6 Yoga is interesting and it's _____ very good for you.

15

GRAMMAR: love, like, hate, enjoy, don't mind + noun/-ing form

1 Complete the text with the -ing form of the verbs in brackets.

> I love ¹_____ (live) with my family! We're all very happy. My dad enjoys ²_____ (drive) his taxi for work every day. My mum's very busy so I don't mind ³_____ (make) breakfast for my little sister and ⁴_____ (take) her to the park sometimes. My brother, Pat, loves ⁵_____ (run) in the park and he really likes ⁶_____ (swim) in the outside pool there – but he hates ⁷_____ (go) to school! At weekends we all enjoy ⁸_____ (be) together. Sometimes I like to be alone though. I love ⁹_____ (sit) with a book or ¹⁰_____ (plan) my future!

2 Complete the sentences with love / not like / hate / enjoy / don't mind + -ing form of the verbs in the box.

study	help	meet	work	spend
play	visit	relax	watch	eat

1 Do you _____ time with your family at the weekend? ☺
2 I _____ vegetables, but I like chips more! ☹
3 My sister _____ Maths and never does her homework. ☹☹
4 Do you _____ in the evening after work? ☺
5 We _____ our friends for coffee in the new café in town. ☺☺
6 Jaime _____ the dentist so he doesn't go very often. ☹☹
7 His uncle makes cars. He _____ in a factory. ☹
8 They _____ their mum with the shopping and cooking. ☺
9 I _____ films at home, but I go to the cinema every week. ☹
10 Does your brother _____ online games? ☺☺

VOCABULARY: Activities (2)

3 Order the letters to make words for activities.

1 OG PSHOPNIG
_____
2 SITIV A LLAGYRE
_____
3 LYAP HET LINVIO
_____
4 OG GLIBWON
_____
5 OD GOYA
_____
6 HEAV A CINCIP
_____
7 APLY LOVELYBLLA
_____
8 ISITV STERILAVE
_____

4 Complete the sentences with the correct verbs.

1 What great weather! Do you want to _____ a barbecue?
2 When it rains on holiday, I like to _____ a museum.
3 I never _____ golf – I think it's a boring game.
4 My girlfriend loves to _____ swimming, but I hate the water!
5 I don't have time to cook, so I often _____ a takeaway for dinner.
6 I want to _____ dancing tonight. There's a great DJ playing!
7 Do you want to _____ cycling at the weekend?
8 His niece wants to learn to _____ karate next year.

PRONUNCIATION: -ing forms

5 ▶ 3.2 Say the sentences. How do we say the -ing forms? Listen, check and repeat.

1 I don't mind playing tennis.
2 We love visiting our grandmother.
3 I don't like being late.
4 I love reading stories.
5 I like running.
6 I hate watching TV.
7 I don't mind going to school.
8 I enjoy doing sport.

SPEAKING: Accepting or declining an invitation

1 Look at the clocks and write the times.

1 It's _____.
2 It's _____.
3 It's _____.
4 It's _____.
5 _____.
6 _____.
7 _____.
8 _____.

2 ▶3.3 Listen to the conversation between two friends. Are the sentences true or false?

1	Pablo suggests going for a walk.	True	False
2	Sara accepts Pablo's invitation for tonight.	True	False
3	Sara must visit her grandfather.	True	False
4	Pablo suggests tomorrow morning.	True	False
5	They agree to meet at one o'clock.	True	False

3 ▶3.3 Complete the lines from the conversation with the words in the box. Then listen again and check.

how   let's   can't   time
say   about   plans   want

1 Do you have _____ after work today?
2 Do you _____ to go to the cinema with me?
3 Tonight? Oh, I'm sorry, I _____.
4 What _____ tomorrow?
5 _____ about having lunch with me?
6 Great, _____ go together.
7 What _____ is good for you?
8 Let's _____ one o'clock.

4 Match 1–5 with a–e to make conversations.

1 Do you want to come to my birthday party on Saturday? ____
2 Would you like to come to the match with me? I've got two tickets. ____
3 How about going to the new burger restaurant together? ____
4 Do you want to have coffee together later? ____
5 Are you free for lunch today? ____

a I'd love to, but I don't eat meat. Sorry!
b Cool! I love football.
c Sure!
d Yes, I'd love to!
e Saturday? I'm sorry, I can't.

5 ▶3.4 Listen and check. Then say if the people accept (A) or decline (D) the invitations in each conversation.

1 ____
2 ____
3 ____
4 ____
5 ____

6 ▶3.4 Listen again and repeat the conversations in exercise 4. Copy the intonation to sound enthusiastic or sorry.

3 REVIEW and PRACTICE

HOME   BLOG   PODCASTS   ABOUT   CONTACT

Tom and Sam talk about a family business.

LISTENING

1 ▶ 3.5 Listen to the podcast about a family business called 'Swish'. Number a–h in the order you hear them (1–8).

a brother _____
b sisters _____
c mother _____
d grandmother _____
e grandfather _____
f cousins _____
g sister-in-law _____
h aunts _____

2 ▶ 3.5 Listen again and choose the correct answers.

1 Why do people enjoy going to Swish?
 a The haircuts are very cheap.
 b The hairdressers are friendly.
 c There's a nice atmosphere.

2 How many family members does Mila think work in the hairdresser?
 a ten
 b eleven
 c twelve

3 How many aunts does Mila have?
 a two
 b three
 c four

4 What does Mila do at Swish?
 a She cuts hair.
 b She makes coffee.
 c She does lots of different things.

5 Does the family enjoy working together?
 a sometimes
 b usually
 c always

6 Why are there sometimes problems?
 a because of money
 b because of customers
 c because they are busy

READING

1 Read the blog on page 19 about spending time with your family. Write R (Roberto), M (Mariella) or B (both). Who:

1 doesn't like playing golf? _____
2 is busy at work? _____
3 likes going out with friends? _____
4 doesn't enjoy going dancing? _____
5 doesn't like shopping? _____
6 goes cycling three times a month? _____

2 Are the sentences true (T) or false (F)?

1 Roberto doesn't like music. _____
2 Mariella and Roberto hardly ever talk together. _____
3 Mariella plays golf with her friends. _____
4 Roberto likes playing golf with his daughter. _____
5 Roberto has a lot of free time. _____
6 Mariella and Roberto sometimes cycle to the beach. _____
7 Mariella talks to her father about school. _____
8 Roberto enjoys going cycling with Mariella. _____

3 Circle the adverbs and expressions of frequency in the blog.

REVIEW and PRACTICE 3

HOME BLOG PODCASTS ABOUT CONTACT

Guest blogger Simon writes about how a father and a daughter spend time together.

Family time

In today's busy world, it isn't always easy for families to spend time together. So why not try doing your mother's, father's, son's or daughter's hobby with them? Read about how Mariella and her dad, Roberto, enjoy some free time together.

Mariella

My dad plays golf three times a week. He's always at the golf course. I don't know why! I don't think it's a great sport – you don't run, there's no music and I don't like the clothes people wear!

I don't see my dad very often and sometimes I don't know what to talk about with him. That's why I like coming here together, because there's always something to talk about – where the golf ball is going, for example! When we're at home, I'm usually on my phone talking to friends. But I never look at my phone when we play golf!

I play golf with dad about once a week. I don't really like it very much, but I like being with him and I know he enjoys it, too.

Roberto

I have a very busy job and I hardly ever have free time. But Mariella doesn't often talk to me. She has a lot of friends and she enjoys going out with them. And she never stops talking on her phone! She loves going dancing, too – but it's not my favourite thing! It's probably a bit boring to go out with your father. So it's great that Mariella plays golf with me. It's very special.

Mariella loves cycling, so we also go cycling together three times a month. Mariella always decides where to go. Sometimes we take our bikes to the beach, sometimes to the hills. We often talk – usually about things like school or work. Sometimes we talk about our favourite music. I'm happy to do Mariella's hobby with her. But I hope she never asks me to go shopping with her. I hate going shopping!

19

UNIT 4 Home and away

4A LANGUAGE

GRAMMAR: Prepositions of time

1 Complete the sentences with the words in the box.

| in (x2) on (x2) to at (x2) from |

1 _____ Friday nights, I usually have a takeaway.
2 The bank is open _____ 10 a.m. to 4 p.m.
3 School is always closed _____ August.
4 _____ the winter, I don't go out very often.
5 We study a lot _____ the weekend.
6 I'm always tired _____ Monday morning.
7 Where were you _____ midnight last night?
8 The outdoor swimming pool is open from May _____ October.

2 Complete the text with prepositions of time.

A typical day? Well, I usually get up ¹_____ 7 a.m., but ²_____ summer it's lighter, so I get up earlier – maybe 6.30 a.m. I have a job in a café – I serve food to customers.
I work ³_____ 10 a.m. ⁴_____ 6 p.m. every day in the week – ⁵_____ Monday ⁶_____ Friday. After work, ⁷_____ 6 p.m., I usually meet my friends. ⁸_____ Friday nights we go to a restaurant or to the cinema. ⁹_____ July, the café is closed for one month, so I don't work at all. It's also closed ¹⁰_____ Christmas. Then, my typical day is very different!

VOCABULARY: Daily routine verbs

3 Order the verbs 1–8 to make a typical day.

a get home _____
b leave work _____
c have dinner _____
d go to bed _____
e have breakfast _____
f go to work _____
g go to sleep _____
h get up _____

4 Order the letters to make daily routine verbs.

1 I **egt deserds** after a big breakfast.
2 Do you watch TV before you **og ot loshoc**?
3 My brother doesn't often **veah clunh** because he's busy.
4 Yolanda likes to **kwae pu** early and read a magazine.
5 On Sunday, before I **teg pu**, I have a cup of coffee.
6 Does he **vahe a roshew** every morning?
7 Our mum sometimes **sha a hatb** before bed.
8 When they **evale closho** they play in the park.

PRONUNCIATION: Sentence stress

5 ▶ 4.1 Read the sentences. Which words are stressed? Listen, check and repeat.

1 I get up at eleven o'clock.
2 I go to school from nine o'clock to three o'clock.
3 We have breakfast at 7.30.
4 He cycles to work in the summer.
5 I play football on Saturday afternoons.
6 She wakes up at eight.

SKILLS 4B

LISTENING: Listening for the main idea

1 ▶ 4.2 Listen to a conversation about Hong Kong. Tick (✓) the different types of weather you hear.

a ____

b ____

c ____

d ____

e ____

f ____

2 ▶ 4.2 Listen again. Are the sentences true (T) or false (F)?

1 The weather is always the same in Hong Kong. ____
2 Fiona doesn't like hot weather. ____
3 Fiona is a student. ____
4 It never rains in Hong Kong. ____
5 Typhoons bring bad weather. ____

3 Complete the weather words for a–f in exercise 1.

a s_____g
b s_____y
c r_____g
d f_____y
e w_____y
f c_____y

4 Order the letters to make seasons. Which words from exercise 3 describe the weather in your country in each season?

1 RETWIN _____
2 GRINPS _____
3 UNMATU _____
4 REMUMS _____

5 ▶ 4.3 Read the sentences. <u>Underline</u> the words which you think will be stressed. Listen and check.

1 What's the climate like there?
2 There are four seasons.
3 The weather is too hot for me.
4 It always rains here!
5 Is Hong Kong a beautiful city?

21

4C LANGUAGE

GRAMMAR: Present continuous

1 Choose the correct options to complete the sentences.

1 I ____ a great time in New York.
 a has b having c 'm having

2 'Where's Peter?' 'He ____ his mother at the moment.'
 a 's helping b helps c are helping

3 'Are we eating lunch here?' 'No, we ____.'
 a don't b aren't c isn't

4 Where ____ you going right now?
 a is b are c do

5 I'm ____ enjoying this film.
 a doesn't b not c no

6 Are you ____ to the party on Friday?
 a come b comes c coming

7 Laila's ____ tonight, so she isn't here.
 a work b works c working

8 ____ they having a karate lesson today?
 a Do b Are c Is

9 'Is he listening to the radio?' 'No, he ____.'
 a is b doesn't c isn't

10 They ____ going clubbing in town this week.
 a aren't b not c don't

2 Order the words to make statements and questions.

1 in / we / the classroom / sitting / are / now
_____

2 their holiday / India / aren't / they / spending / in
_____

3 today / are / enjoying / the children / school
_____?

4 she / the moment / listening / at / isn't
_____

5 visiting / you / this week / are / new places
_____?

6 right / is / now / snowing / it
_____?

7 walking / today / not / the dog / I'm
_____

8 camping / he / is / this year / going
_____

PRONUNCIATION: Linking consonants and vowels

3 ▶ 4.4 <u>Underline</u> the words that are linked. Listen, check and repeat.

1 What are you doing tomorrow?
2 I'm going away next weekend.
3 She's eating her breakfast.
4 It isn't very warm today.
5 I'm getting up late tomorrow.
6 He's asking his teacher.

4 Write sentences to describe what the people (1–8) in the picture are doing.

22

SKILLS 4D

WRITING: Describing a photo

Hey Rob,

How are you? I'm having a great time in London. I'm doing summer school – I love learning English! The weather isn't very hot and it rains a lot, but ¹_____'s good weather for learning and sightseeing.

I'm really busy – there's so much to do! Lessons start at 9 a.m. and ²_____ finish at 1 p.m. I usually get up early and go for a walk before breakfast. I learn English with the other students all morning, then ³_____ stop for lunch. After lunch, we all go into the centre of London to see the sights. In the evening we have dinner together. Then we go to the park or play football.

I'm sending you a few photos. In this photo, I'm playing football with my new friend, George. George is from Serbia – ⁴_____'s really good at sport. This is a photo of my classroom with my English teacher, Joanna. ⁵_____'s really funny and I enjoy her lessons. Here's a photo of my classmates in the park – ⁶_____'s a beautiful place to relax.

Are you in London at the moment? Can we meet some afternoon?

See you soon,

Fernando

1 Read Fernando's email. Complete 1–6 with the correct pronouns.

2 Number a–e in the order Fernando does the things (1–5).

   a describes his daily routine _____
   b asks Rob to meet him _____
   c talks about the weather _____
   d describes some photographs _____
   e asks Rob a friendly question _____

3 Complete the sentences with the correct words.

   1 In _____ photo, we're playing in the park.
   2 This photo is _____ my friend George.
   3 _____ is a photo of my teacher, Joanna.
   4 _____ this photo, we're having lunch.
   5 Here's _____ photo of London.
   6 This photo _____ of the other students in my class.

4 You are at a sports camp. Write an email to a friend. Use personal pronouns to avoid repeating words and names.

Talk about:
- the weather
- your daily routine
- some photos and what you are doing in them.

4 REVIEW and PRACTICE

Tom and Sam talk about sleep.

LISTENING

1 ▶ 4.5 Listen to the podcast about sleep. Tick (✓) the things Dr Patel talks about.

a using a computer ____
b lunch ____
c doing yoga ____
d teenagers ____
e having a bath ____
f having a shower ____
g watching TV ____
h breakfast ____

2 ▶ 4.5 Listen again. Does Dr Patel say the things below? Choose Yes or No.

1	Most teenagers don't get enough sleep.	Yes	No
2	Most teenagers need eight hours sleep a night.	Yes	No
3	Dr Patel eats a big lunch.	Yes	No
4	Dr Patel has dinner late at night.	Yes	No
5	He has a bath every evening.	Yes	No
6	He goes to bed after eleven o'clock.	Yes	No
7	He only works on his computer until six o'clock.	Yes	No
8	The light from your phone can stop you relaxing.	Yes	No

READING

1 Read the blog on page 25 about the weather in two different countries. Match headings 1–5 with paragraphs A–E.

1 Different weather, different clothes ____
2 Making new friends in a new country ____
3 Sport at home and away ____
4 Different lives in two countries ____
5 Summer and winter weather ____

2 Tick (✓) the true sentences.

1 Patrice is a student from Canada. ____
2 He's spending Christmas in Australia. ____
3 He thinks life in Australia is similar to life in Canada. ____
4 He's wearing warm clothes at the beach today. ____
5 He hates the winter in Canada. ____
6 The weather in Canada is very different in summer and winter. ____
7 Patrice doesn't have many friends in Australia. ____
8 He never goes surfing in Canada. ____

3 Circle the weather and the seasons vocabulary in the blog.

REVIEW and PRACTICE 4

HOME   BLOG   PODCASTS   ABOUT   CONTACT

 Guest blogger Marc writes about the weather in different countries.

NORTH AND SOUTH

What's the weather like in your country? Do you think the weather changes how you feel? What happens when people move from a hot country to a cold country, or from a cold place to somewhere really hot? Twenty-year-old Patrice Chiffre told me about moving from Canada to Australia.

A I come from Calgary, a city in Canada, but now I'm studying at university in Australia. The weather in these countries isn't the same at all! And I think it changes how people live and work in these places.

C Where I'm living in Australia at the moment, there is a wet season and a dry season. The wet season is really hot, and the dry season is a little colder. But at home in Canada, the winters are long, dark and really cold. The short and sunny summers bring a big change, so people often eat more healthily, do more exercise and get up early in the morning. I love the summers in Canada – they are full of energy, festivals and parties!

D People spend a lot of time outside in Australia, so it's easy to meet people and make new friends. Of course it's different in Canada, especially in winter. People stay inside more, and don't see their friends very often. I'm meeting lots of new people here in Australia!

B First, the months and seasons aren't the same. In December in Canada, people wear warm coats and hats and some people have Christmas dinner next to a big fire. But in Australia, January is summer and July is winter. Today is the beginning of February and everyone is wearing T-shirts and shorts. I'm eating lunch by the sea with my friends and we're enjoying the sunny weather! People often spend Christmas at the beach here.

E One thing I love about Canada is all the snow and ice we have in winter. I love going skiing, too. It hardly ever snows here in Australia, but I enjoy going surfing – that's something I can't do at home!

25

UNIT 5

What are you wearing?

5A LANGUAGE

GRAMMAR: Present simple and present continuous

1 Choose the correct options to complete the sentences.

1 Ramona is Spanish. She *is coming from / comes from* Spain.
2 My aunt *doesn't work / isn't working* near her home.
3 *I eat / I'm eating* a big breakfast every morning.
4 'Where is Katia?' 'There she is. *She's wearing / She wears* a blue jacket.'
5 Hello! *Are you looking / Do you look* for me?
6 We *don't visit / aren't visiting* our grandparents very often.
7 *Is he watching / Does he watch* TV at the moment?
8 They *aren't selling / don't sell* magazines in this shop.

2 Complete the conversation with the present simple or present continuous form of the verbs in brackets.

Andy Hi! I'm Andy. ¹_____ (you/have) a good time?
Mara Yes, it's a great party! My name's Mara.
Andy Hi Mara! Where ² _____ (you/come from)?
Mara I'm from Brazil, but I ³ _____ (study) in London this summer. What about you?
Andy I'm Welsh, but I ⁴ _____ (not live) in Wales. I ⁵ _____ (work) here with my parents for a few months.
Mara That's interesting! What ⁶ _____ (they/do)?
Andy They ⁷ _____ (repair) cars. We ⁸ _____ (not make) a lot of money, but my mum ⁹ _____ (enjoy) working with the family!
Mara That's brilliant! My mum ¹⁰ _____ (not have) a job at the moment, but she wants to be a singer!

VOCABULARY: Clothes and ordinal numbers

3 Match definitions 1–8 with clothes a–h.

1 You might wear these on your legs at the beach. ____
2 This makes your neck warm on a cold day. ____
3 You can put these on your hands when it's cold. ____
4 Men often wear this at work. ____
5 You need these on your feet in the snow. ____
6 You can wear this on your head in summer or winter. ____
7 You wear this around the top of your trousers. ____
8 When it's hot and sunny, people wear these on their feet. ____

a sandals
b belt
c hat
d gloves
e scarf
f shorts
g tie
h boots

4 Write the words next to the ordinal numbers.

1 11th _____
2 3rd _____
3 12th _____
4 29th _____
5 40th _____
6 36th _____
7 28th _____
8 19th _____
9 31st _____
10 14th _____

PRONUNCIATION: Dates

5 ▶5.1 Underline the stressed words. Listen, check and repeat.

1 It's May the fifteenth.
2 It's December the sixth.
3 It's the thirtieth of November.
4 It's the eleventh of April.
5 It's October the twelfth.
6 It's the twenty-third of June.
7 It's the sixteenth of February.
8 It's July the twenty-ninth.
9 It's the fourteenth of January.
10 It's August the thirty-first.

Skills 5B

READING: Identifying facts and opinions

ALL ABOUT CLOTHES ...

I'm Marta and I'm a fashion blogger from Chile. I love making my own clothes and posting pictures of them on this blog!

A I write my blog at home. I need to wear warm clothes because my house is cold. In this picture, I'm wearing my favourite working clothes – I call this my uniform! I think this dress is ¹*tianlrilb* – it's really long and it keeps me warm, too. My best friend makes jewellery – in this picture I'm wearing one of her necklaces.

B I love walking and there are lots of mountains in Chile. I often go hiking at the weekend. Here I am in my favourite hat and walking trousers. I think they're ²*tearg!*

C I'm not just a fashion blogger! I also have a part-time job. I work as a waitress in a café near my home. I can wear what I like because there isn't a uniform. I usually wear this black skirt and smart white top because I think it looks ³*lvoyel*. Do you like my shoes?

D This is my ⁴*eautfilub* little brother! He's only five years old. I really like making clothes for him. He's wearing green trousers and a T-shirt because these are his favourite clothes.

E The clothes I make aren't always good. This dress is horrible – it's ⁵*sranibregams!* It's too big for me and it's also too short. It's ⁶*fulwa*, I know, but everyone makes mistakes!

1

2

3

4

5

1 Read Marta's blog. Match paragraphs A–E with pictures 1–5.

A _____
B _____
C _____
D _____
E _____

2 Order the letters in 1–6 in the blog to make adjectives.

1 _____
2 _____
3 _____
4 _____
5 _____
6 _____

3 Read the sentences from some of Marta's other blog posts. Are they opinion (O) or fact (F)?

1 I agree that shopping for clothes is boring. _____
2 There are 25 clothes shops in my town. _____
3 I think that my big brother's clothes are terrible! _____
4 My birthday is on 23rd June. I want to get some new shoes! _____
5 I don't think that British people have very good clothes. _____
6 My mother has a job as a nurse. _____

5C LANGUAGE

GRAMMAR: *can* and *can't*

1 Complete the sentences with *can* or *can't*.

1. I _____ see it because I'm not wearing my glasses.
2. '_____ you help me, please?' 'Yes, of course!'
3. 'Where is the nearest café?' 'I'm sorry, we're not from here. We _____ tell you.'
4. Anita is a great photographer. She _____ take really good photos.
5. 'Can Miguel cook Chinese food?' 'No, he _____.'
6. '_____ they speak French?' 'Yes, a little.'
7. Are you hungry? You _____ have some of my pizza if you like.
8. You _____ buy this book, but you can download it.
9. 'Can you see the sea from your house?' 'Yes, we _____.'
10. She can go to the club tonight, but she _____ stay too late.

2 Complete the sentences with *can* or *can't* and the verbs in the box.

| run | read | teach | come | play | go out |
| hear | understand | ask | borrow | | |

1. '_____ I _____ you a question?' 'Yes, what is it?'
2. Sarah _____ _____ football, but she likes watching it.
3. I'm going to Italy next week. _____ you _____ me some Italian words?
4. 'Can you _____ this letter?' 'No, I _____. The writing is really small.'
5. I _____ _____ very fast because I'm wearing sandals!
6. Alina has a lot of homework, so she _____ _____ tonight.
7. _____ I _____ your book? It looks really interesting.
8. They _____ _____ to my party on Saturday – they're on holiday.
9. 'Can you _____ that noise?' 'Yes, I _____ – what is it?'
10. I _____ _____ you – you're speaking too fast.

VOCABULARY: Hobbies

3 Match the two parts of the sentences.

1. My friend Anita makes _____
2. Our grandmother collects _____
3. His English teacher plays _____
4. Her sister takes _____
5. What does he draw _____
6. Can you bake _____

a pictures of?
b really good photos of animals.
c a cake for my birthday?
d jewellery like bracelets and necklaces.
e coins. She has over a thousand!
f the drums in a band.

4 Complete the sentences with the correct verbs.

1. At school, we _____ blogs about what we are learning.
2. Daniel _____ pictures of his girlfriend in beautiful colours.
3. My sister _____ online games for hours.
4. Can you _____ chess? Do you want to learn?
5. Costa's aunt wants to _____ him a jumper for the winter.
6. Not many people _____ stamps these days.

PRONUNCIATION: *can* and *can't*

5 ▶ 5.2 Say the sentences. How do we say *can* and *can't*? Listen, check and repeat.

1. I can't sew clothes. Can you?
2. 'Can you speak Chinese?' 'Yes, I can.'
3. John can't sing, but he can play the drums.
4. My mum can cook really well.
5. I can dance, but I can't sing.
6. My dad can leave work early this week.
7. 'Can your brother play the violin?' 'No, he can't.'
8. You can't buy a new top today.

SKILLS 5D

SPEAKING: Offering help

1 ▶5.3 Listen to Tim talking about shopping for his holiday. Tick (✓) the clothes you hear.

a coat ____
b boots ____
c scarf ____
d shirt ____
e gloves ____
f jumper ____
g sandals ____
h shorts ____
i socks ____
j T-shirt ____

2 Complete the questions with the words in the box. Then match them with answers a–f below.

| sell | in | colours | pay | changing | much |

1 Do you have it _____ blue? ____
2 Do you _____ scarves? ____
3 What _____ are there? ____
4 How _____ is this green one? ____
5 Where are the men's _____ rooms, please? ____
6 Can I _____ with this credit card? ____

a They're all 30 euros.
b I'll show you.
c We do, yes.
d Just a moment, I'll check. Yes, here you are.
e Certainly, sir.
f We have these in black, red and green.

3 ▶5.3 Listen and check.

4 ▶5.4 Listen to 5 conversations. What does the shop assistant do? Choose the correct option.

	asks if the customer needs help	says that he/she will do something
1		
2		
3		
4		
5		

5 ▶5.4 Read the conversations. What do you think the shop assistant says? Then listen again and check.

1
Shop assistant Are you alright? Do you _____ any help?
Customer Yes – do you sell coats?

2
Shop assistant Can I help _____?
Customer Yes, please. How much are these pyjamas?

3
Customer Can I pay with this credit card?
Shop assistant Just a moment, I'll _____.

4
Customer Where are the men's changing rooms?
Shop assistant I'll _____ you where they are.

5
Customer Do you have this suit in medium?
Shop assistant _____ me ask my colleague.

6 ▶5.4 Listen again. Repeat what the shop assistant says.

29

5 REVIEW and PRACTICE

HOME BLOG **PODCASTS** ABOUT CONTACT

Tom and Sam talk about a music competition.

LISTENING

1 🔊 5.5 Listen to the podcast about a music competition. Choose the correct answers.

1 How old is Tony Pia?
   a 17
   b 18
   c 20
2 What instrument can Tony play well?
   a the drums
   b the piano
   c the guitar
3 When is the final of the music competition?
   a 30 June
   b 30 January
   c 13 June

2 🔊 5.5 Listen again. Complete the sentences with one or two words.

1 The competition is called Young Drummer of _____.
2 Young people from all over _____ enter the competition.
3 Tony is feeling a bit _____.
4 Tony's mum can play the _____.
5 Tony plays the drums every _____.
6 Playing the drums makes Tony feel _____ and full of energy.

READING

1 Read the blog on page 31 about what to wear for a job interview. Answer the questions.

1 What is Angela Santo's job?
2 What is Norbert Szil's job?
3 Which person's clothes does Angela prefer?
4 Which person's clothes does Norbert prefer?

2 Are the sentences correct? Choose Yes or No.

1	Angela and Norbert like Jo's hat.	Yes	No
2	Angela doesn't like Jo's scarf.	Yes	No
3	Norbert likes Jo's scarf and top.	Yes	No
4	Norbert thinks Dan looks good.	Yes	No
5	Angela thinks Dan is wearing great clothes for an interview.	Yes	No
6	Angela likes all Isa's clothes.	Yes	No
7	Angela thinks skirts are better than trousers for an interview.	Yes	No
8	Norbert thinks Isa's clothes are good for a job in fashion.	Yes	No

3 Circle the clothes vocabulary in the blog.

REVIEW and PRACTICE 5

HOME   BLOG   PODCASTS   ABOUT   CONTACT

Guest blogger Ethan hears about wearing the right clothes.

Dress for success

You have an interview for the job of your dreams. Congratulations! So, what are you thinking of wearing on the big day? It can be easy to make bad choices. Angela Santo is a hotel manager and Norbert Szil has a fashion business. They tell me how to dress for success.

Jo

Angela I'm not at all sure about this one. Why is she wearing a hat?' I don't think that hats are a great idea – not for a job interview. And I don't think the scarf is very tidy. It looks a little informal, too.

Norbert I agree with Angela about the hat. I don't agree with her about the rest of the clothes, though. This woman is wearing very smart clothes and I think the scarf and top are good together. She looks cool!

Dan

Norbert This man is carrying an old case. It's not at all smart! It looks awful! I think he's wearing a suit, shirt and tie, but are those trainers on his feet? This is never a good look, but for a job interview it's terrible!

Angela I agree with Norbert. This man does not look smart. Are you sure he's going to a job interview?

Isa

Angela This woman has got it right! The skirt is great – not too long or short – and it's dark blue, which is a great colour for interviews. She's wearing a nice jacket, too. Suits are great for interviews, and women can wear trouser suits or skirt suits.

Norbert Is this woman looking for a job in a bank? I think she'll do well. There's just one thing – I can't imagine her working in fashion. Her clothes are a bit boring. Some colour is always a great thing, and how about some jewellery?

UNIT 6 Homes and cities

6A LANGUAGE

GRAMMAR: *there is/there are, some/any* and prepositions of place

1 Complete the text with the words in the box.

| there are | are | are there | there's |
| is | any | there | some |

So, this is my bedroom – I really like it! [1]_____ a window by my bed, so I can see outside. Opposite the bed is a TV. I love watching TV in bed at night! [2]_____ some cupboards, too, for my clothes. [3]_____ any shelves? Yes, there [4]_____ – look! There are [5]_____ shelves beside the bed. There aren't [6]_____ books on them because I don't like reading. [7]_____ are lots of DVDs though. And [8]_____ there a desk? No, I do my homework downstairs on the big table!

2 Choose the preposition which is **not** correct.

1 The boy is *in front of / behind / between* the door.
2 The table is *next to / opposite / in* a small window.
3 The big chair is *on / behind / in front of* the cupboard.
4 Is his book *under / between / next to* your shopping bag?
5 My house is *between / under / opposite* the park and the station.
6 Two apples are *in / under / on* the table.
7 Your cat is *behind / on / between* the sofa.
8 Is your flat *next to / between / on* those two shops?
9 Our teacher is *in / next to / in front of* the big desk.
10 Her phone is *behind / in / under* the TV.

VOCABULARY: Rooms and furniture

3 Order the letters to make words for rooms or furniture.

1 Is there a DROBRAWE in your bedroom?
_____
2 There are a lot of old books and toys in the TENSMEAB of our house.
_____
3 When it's sunny I like sitting outside on the YLBCAON.
_____
4 We've got a AGGARE where my parents keep their car.
_____
5 Julia's in the THRABOMO. She's having a shower.
_____
6 Their house has a LITTOE upstairs and one downstairs.
_____

4 Write the words for the definitions.

1 You look at your face in this.
m_____
2 You can wash your clothes in this.
w_____ m_____
3 This is a room at the top of a house.
a_____
4 You walk up and down these.
s_____
5 You eat food here.
d_____ r_____
6 There are often flowers and trees here.
g_____
7 You can do your homework here.
s_____
8 You cook food here.
k_____

PRONUNCIATION: *there's/there are*

5 ▶6.1 Say the sentences. How do we say *there's* and *there are*? Listen again and repeat.

1 There's a bed in the living room.
2 There are some chairs next to the table.
3 Is there a sofa in your bedroom?
4 Are there any shelves? No, there aren't.
5 There are five tables in their house.
6 Is there any food in the cupboard?
7 There's a cooker in his room.
8 There isn't a hall in his apartment.

32

SKILLS 6B

LISTENING: Identifying key points

1 ▶6.2 Listen to a TV show about houses. Tick (✓) the key points the speakers talk about.

a the furniture ____
b the colours of the rooms ____
c spending time with the family ____
d the garden ____
e the size of the house ____

2 ▶6.2 Listen again. Complete the sentences.

1 The windows are really big and _____.
2 At first, the house had two _____.
3 Loretta has _____ children.
4 The presenter thinks their furniture is really _____.
5 Loretta's husband really likes _____ furniture.
6 Loretta painted the bathroom and _____.
7 The furniture was _____ expensive.
8 Loretta loves sitting on the _____ in the summer.

3 Read the sentences. Write the full form or contracted form of the underlined words.

1 He's very busy at work. _____
2 There is a picture on the wall. _____
3 The table is near the window. _____
4 It's a sunny day today. _____
5 I do not like vegetables. _____
6 I'm nineteen years old. _____
7 She is not very friendly. _____
8 They're not cheap at all. _____

4 Put the adjectives in the box into seven pairs of opposite meanings.

| clean light narrow uncomfortable dirty |
| cheap modern quiet heavy expensive |
| traditional wide noisy comfortable |

1 _____ _____
2 _____ _____
3 _____ _____
4 _____ _____
5 _____ _____
6 _____ _____
7 _____ _____

33

6C LANGUAGE

GRAMMAR: Modifiers

1 Choose the correct options to complete the sentences.

1 I love Suzy's house! It's ___ beautiful.
   a quite   b really   c not very

2 I don't like that dress – it's ___ nice.
   a quite   b not at all   c very

3 'Do you like this music?' 'It's ___ good, but it's not my favourite.'
   a not very   b not at all   c quite

4 We don't want any dinner, thanks. We're ___ hungry.
   a really   b not very   c very

5 Everyone likes Laura. She's ___ friendly.
   a not very   b really   c quite

6 'Can you clean your bedroom? It's ___ tidy.'
   a not at all   b very   c really

7 'Can they speak English well?' 'They can speak it ___ well, but they want to get better.'
   a very   b not at all   c quite

8 She's ___ good at sport. She often wins competitions!
   a not at all   b not very   c very

2 Order the words to make sentences.

1 sunny / not / today / it's / at all

2 quite / good student / is / Emile / a

3 really / costumes / your / colourful / are

4 friendly / her uncle / very / is / not

5 goes / early / to bed / Paola / very

6 not / my / warm / are / gloves / at all

VOCABULARY: Places in a city

3 Order the letters to make words for places in a city.

1 QUESOM

2 TREHEAT

3 METNUNOM

4 HETACLADR

5 QERUAS

6 TRAPATEMN KLOCB

7 HRUCHC

8 NORETCC LALH

4 Complete the words.

1 My mum goes to the m_____t every morning to buy fruit and vegetables.

2 We live in an old city, so there aren't many s_____s or other tall buildings.

3 My sister loves reading. She's always at the l_____y in town.

4 There's a small s_____m here. They play rugby every weekend.

5 His brother-in-law's an accountant. He works in an o_____e b_____k.

6 In my village there's a b_____e over the river.

PRONUNCIATION: Sentence stress

5 ▶ 6.3 <u>Underline</u> the stressed words in the sentences. Listen, check and repeat.

1 That chair isn't very comfortable.
2 Her grandparents' house is quite modern.
3 It's a very famous painting.
4 That restaurant isn't at all expensive.
5 Our balcony is always really sunny.
6 This is quite a heavy table.
7 The restaurant is very traditional.

WRITING: Topic sentences

SKILLS 6D

A _____ It's on the River Guadalquivir, but it's quite far from the sea. It's a busy and lively place with a population of 700,000.

B _____ You can visit museums, art centres, cinemas and theatres. The Plaza de España is a very famous place. It was built in 1928 and is really popular with tourists. If you like being active, you can play football or golf at the parks and sports centres. There are lots of great places to go walking, too.

C _____ There are really lovely restaurants where you can get delicious tapas and traditional Spanish food. You must try the delicious meat, Secreto Ibérico – it's fantastic!

D _____ A lot of tourists come to the April Fair every spring. This celebration takes place next to the river – it's a wonderful party. There is horse-riding, music and women wearing colourful flamenco dresses.

E _____ Nicer times to visit are spring and autumn, when it's sunny and a little bit cooler.

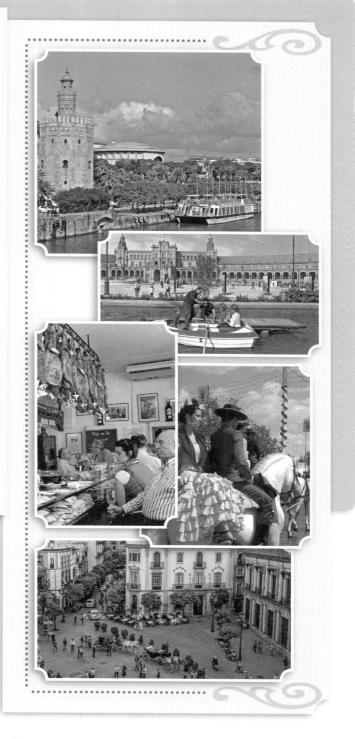

1 Read the text about Seville. Match paragraphs A–E with topic sentences 1–5.

1 If you visit Seville in the summer, it can be very hot. ___
2 Seville is also well known for its festivals. ___
3 You can always find something good to eat in this city. ___
4 Seville is a famous Spanish city. ___
5 There are so many things for tourists to see and do in Seville. ___

2 Complete each sentence about Rome with one word.

1 Rome is the _____ city of Italy.
2 More than 2.5 million people _____ there.
3 Walking is a great _____ to see the sights.
4 There are wonderful _____ of the city from the top of the Gianicolo hill.
5 If _____ like historical sights, go to the Colosseum.
6 There are also lots of really good _____ to eat.

3 Write about a city you know well. Begin each paragraph with a topic sentence. Include the following information:

Paragraph 1: Where is the city?
Paragraph 2: What can you do there?
Paragraph 3: What special events or festivals are there?
Paragraph 4: Where can you go to eat?
Paragraph 5: When is the best time to visit?

35

6 REVIEW and PRACTICE

HOME   BLOG   PODCASTS   ABOUT   CONTACT

Tom and Sam talk about Sally and José's house.

LISTENING

1 ▶ 6.4 Listen to the podcast about Sally and José's house. What is unusual about it?

a There is no furniture.
b There are two houses inside it.
c It's very untidy.

2 ▶ 6.4 Listen again. Are the sentences true (T) or false (F)?

1 Sally and José live in the country. ____
2 They don't like each other. ____
3 They can't live together. ____
4 Sally goes to bed late. ____
5 José gets up early. ____
6 They are both clean and tidy. ____
7 They have the same rooms. ____
8 José doesn't see Sally every day. ____

3 ▶ 6.4 Listen again and tick (✓) the parts of the house that Sally and José mention.

1 garden ____
2 dining room ____
3 kitchen ____
4 living room ____
5 bedroom ____
6 bathroom ____
7 basement ____
8 hall ____

READING

1 Read the blog on page 37 about Buenos Aires. Match paragraphs A–E with pictures 1–5.

1 ____
2 ____
3 ____
4 ____
5 ____

2 Choose the correct options to complete the sentences.

1 El Ateneo Grand Splendid doesn't sell
   a books.
   b furniture.
   c food and drink.

2 You can watch sport at
   a San Telmo.
   b La Poesía.
   c La Bombonera.

3 You don't have to pay for
   a the football matches.
   b the walking tours.
   c the coffee at La Poesía.

4 They sell cheap clothes
   a in the park.
   b next to the theatre.
   c at the market.

5 San Telmo has lots of
   a interesting buildings.
   b good places for music.
   c parks.

6 The Street art tour
   a is in one part of the city.
   b is in different parts of the city.
   c starts next to an ice-cream shop.

REVIEW and PRACTICE 6

HOME   BLOG   PODCASTS   ABOUT   CONTACT

Tom and Sam write about Buenos Aires.

The best of Buenos Aires

We asked our readers to tell us about their favourite places in the beautiful city of Buenos Aires. Thanks for all your great ideas. We want to go there – now! We hope you do too when you read our blog!

A El Ateneo Grand Splendid
El Ateneo Grand Splendid is the best bookshop in the world! It's in a beautiful building, which is nearly a hundred years old. There are lots of books, balconies, comfortable chairs and there's a café that sells excellent coffee and cakes. It's perfect for book lovers!

B La Bombonera
Above the houses and shops of La Boca you can find the football stadium. This is where the Boca Junior Football team plays. It's not too expensive to get a ticket for a match, and it's a really exciting place to spend some time.

C City walking tours
Every day there are free walking tours of Buenos Aires, and you can choose to see the city by day or by night. You'll visit modern and traditional buildings, from libraries to cathedrals. There is also a stop at the local market where you can buy clothes, food and drink – clothes are not at all expensive here. The tour begins in the park opposite the National Theatre and finishes in a bar where you can hear some live Argentinian music.

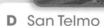

D San Telmo
San Telmo is the oldest part of the city. There are narrow streets full of interesting shops, monuments and some excellent restaurants, too. It's a great place to find an outdoor café, order a coffee and watch the world go past. A very popular café is La Poesía. It's next to a beautiful old church.

E Street art tour
Buenos Aires is famous for street art, and there are some really colourful paintings. The street art tour is a good way to learn about the artists of this amazing place. It takes you all over the city and finishes in a famous ice cream shop. The guides are really friendly too!

Our next blog post is about Egypt. Do you have any useful travel tips? Let us know!

37

WRITING PRACTICE

WRITING: Opening and closing an informal email

Hello Bella,

How are you? I hope everything's okay in Italy.

It's nice to meet you. My name's Andreas and I'm eighteen years old. I'm from Germany, but I'm in the USA at the moment. I'm at a language school to learn English. It's great here, but I don't like the weather – it's very hot!

I speak English every day with my host family. My host mother is a doctor and she doesn't have a lot of free time. She has two sons: Andy and Greg. Greg is eighteen and Andy is sixteen. They are both students.

At the weekend we go shopping or we play sport. Sometimes we go to the cinema – there are some really good cinemas here.

Write soon with your news,

Andreas

1 Read Andreas's email to a penfriend. Complete the sentences.

1 Andreas is from _____.
2 He is eighteen _____ old.
3 At the moment, Andreas is in _____.
4 He _____ the weather there.
5 He _____ sport at the weekends.

2 Complete the sentences with *and*, *but* or *or*.

1 Andreas is German _____ he's eighteen.
2 Andreas can speak German _____ speak English.
3 He's from Germany _____ now he is in the USA.
4 He likes the USA _____ the weather is too hot.
5 He plays sport _____ he goes shopping at the weekend.

3 Are the words and phrases for opening (O) or closing (C) an informal email?

1 Hi   O C
2 See you soon O C
3 Hey   O C
4 Take care   O C
5 Hello   O C
6 Write soon   O C

4 Write an email to a new friend.

- introduce yourself
- say your name, age and where you live
- use informal language to open and close your email

WRITING PRACTICE

WRITING: Describing a photo

Hi Malu,

How are you? How's your new job?

I know you like films, so I'm sending you some photos of me with my film group. We make films together on Tuesday and Friday evenings and we have a lot of fun. We sometimes go to the cinema, too!

Here's a photo of the film club at the cinema – we're watching a horror film! The second photo is of Ella and Sam. They're making a film in the park – it's a comedy film, so they're laughing. Sam is holding the camera in his hand. He makes great films.

See you soon,

Viktor

1 Read Viktor's email. In what order (1–4) does he do things a–d?

   a talk about the film group   _____
   b close the email   _____
   c describe some photos of the film group   _____
   d open the email   _____

2 Viktor has some more photos of the film club. Match the two parts of the sentences.

   1 In this photo I'm with _____
   2 Here's a photo of Ella _____
   3 Here's a photo of _____
   4 In this photo we're _____

   a and Sam with their cameras.
   b my friend, Bruce.
   c sitting in the cinema together.
   d my favourite camera.

3 Complete the sentences with the personal pronouns in the box.

    | I   you   he   she   it   we   they |

   1 This is where the film club meets. _____'s a small café near our college.
   2 Ella works part time. _____'s a waitress in a café.
   3 Ella and Sam sing and make music. _____'re really good actors, too.
   4 I'm with Sam. _____'re talking about ideas for our next film.
   5 Sam has an older brother. _____'s at film school.
   6 What do you and your friends like doing? Do _____ enjoy watching films?
   7 This is my camera. _____ love making films with it!

4 Write an email to a friend about a free-time activity you enjoy. Use the notes to help you plan your email.

   Paragraph 1: Ask your friend how he/she is.
   Paragraph 2: Say what the activity is and why you like it.
   Paragraph 3: Say when you do it and who with.
   Paragraph 4: Describe two or three photos of your activity.

WRITING PRACTICE

WRITING: Topic sentences

Where to buy clothes in Paris

A _____ But where can you go to get the best clothes? It's easy when you know the city. Here are some of my favourite places.

B _____ There are lots of them in many parts of the city and you can find really interesting things. You can buy costumes and jewellery from the 1960s and 1970s – they're cheap, too.

C _____ On the Champs Élysées there are lots of small shops. You can buy beautiful shirts, trousers and jackets. Film stars and pop stars shop there, too!

D _____ The Centre Beaugrenelle is my favourite! It's a wonderful place to meet friends and to go for coffee, too. You can also go to the cinema there.

E _____ There are many great cafés and parks in Paris – you can always find somewhere to relax after shopping! Montmartre is a great area for restaurants!

1 Read the text about clothes shopping in Paris. Match topic sentences 1–6 with paragraphs A–E. There is one extra sentence.

1 If you like old clothes, go to the markets. _____
2 There are also a lot of big shopping centres. _____
3 The best time to go shopping in Paris is in spring. _____
4 Shopping can be hard work sometimes. _____
5 Everyone knows that Paris is a brilliant place for clothes shopping. _____
6 There are also some very expensive shops in Paris. _____

2 Choose the correct options to complete the sentences.

1 There are lots _____ good places to go shopping in my town.
   a on   b of   c at
2 The City Mall is a good place _____ fashionable clothes.
   a in   b of   c for
3 There are wonderful views of the city _____ the top floor of this shopping centre.
   a to   b from   c in
4 If you _____ to find some really different clothes, go to the Saturday market.
   a want   b try   c take
5 Eating at the View Café is a great _____ to finish the day after shopping.
   a time   b way   c part

3 Write a description of some different places to go shopping in your town or city. Begin each paragraph with a topic sentence.

Paragraph 1: Describe the locations.
Paragraph 2: Say what you can buy there.
Paragraph 3: Say when is the best time to visit them.
Paragraph 4: Say what you like about the places.

NOTES

Richmond

58 St Aldates
Oxford
OX1 1ST
United Kingdom

Printed in Mexico
ISBN: 978-84-668-2915-1
CP: 881115
DL: M-29775-2017
© Richmond / Santillana Global S.L. 2017

All rights reserved. No part of this book may be reproduced, stored in a retrieval system or transmitted in any form by any means, electronic, mechanical, photocopying, recording or otherwise, without the prior permission in writing of the Publisher.

Publishing Director: Deborah Tricker
Publisher: Simone Foster
Media Publisher: Sue Ashcroft
Workbook Publisher: Luke Baxter
Editors: Debra Emmett, Helen Ward, Ruth Goodman, Ruth Cox, Tom Hadland, Fiona Hunt, Eleanor Clements, Helen Wendholt
Proofreaders: Peter Anderson, Amanda Leigh, Tas Cooper
Design Manager: Lorna Heaslip
Cover Design: This Ain't Rock'n'Roll, London
Design & Layout: Lorna Heaslip, 320 Design
Photo Researcher: Magdalena Mayo
Learning Curve **video:** Mannic Media
Audio production: Tom, Dick and Debbie, TEFL Audio
App development: The Distance

We would also like to thank the following people for their valuable contribution to writing and developing the material:
Graham Fruen, Bob McLarty, Brigit Viney, Pamela Vittorio (Video Script Writer), Belen Fernandez (App Project Manager), Rob Sved (App Content Creator)

Illustrators:
Simon Clare, Richard Duckett, James Gibbs and Olvind Hovland c/o NB Illustration; Dermot Flynn c/o Dutch Uncle; John Goodwin, Joanna Kerr c/o New Division; John Holcroft; Neal c/o KJA Artists

Photos:
Alicia García; B. Balaguer; C. Pérez; J. Jaime; S. Enríquez; S. Padura; V. Atmán; 123RF; A. G. E. FOTOSTOCK/Pixtal, Fancy; ABB FOTÓGRAFOS; ALAMY/New York City, Johner Images, Josef Polc, Ira Berger, eye35, Geraint Lewis, David Crausby, Peter Usbeck, Nikreates, Joe Vogan, Urbanmyth, AF archive, Cultura RM, Phililp Quirk, Philip Scalia, AGF Srl, Jozef Polc, Roman Babakin, peter dazeley, Hero Images Inc., CRIBER PHOTO, Jim West, studiomonde, Ian Shaw, Zoonar GmbH, Thomas Cockrem, Blend Images, Ian Francis stock, Image Source, Olaf Doering, Peter Schatz, ONOKY - Photononstop, Roger Bamber, Tetra Images, Vadym Drobot, Aurora Photos, B Christopher, Brendan Duffy, Chloe Johnson, Pablo Paul, Y.Levy, Steven May, Michael Dwyer, STOCKFOLIO®, age fotostock, D. Hurst, Milan Machaty, aberCPC, Minkimo, View Stock, robertharding, Kevin Britland, Juan Aunion, REUTERS, Jochen Tack, Keith Leighton, Jorge Tutor, Peter Forsberg, Radharc Images, Fredrick Kippe, Danita Delimont, Francis Specker, Joerg Boethling, Loop Images Ltd, Wavebreak Media, Bill Bachmann, David Kilpatrick, Dzianis Apolka, Jan Halaska, Perry van Munster, Bernardo Galmarini, Jose Luis Stephens, Andrey Kekyalyaynen, Homer Sykes archive, Konstantin Kalishko, Jonathan Smith, dpa picture alliance, Cultura Creative (RF), Jeff Greenberg 6 of 6, World History Archive, mauritius images GmbH, SIBSA Digital Pvt. Ltd., JTB Media Creation, INC., Henry Westheim Photography, Richard Wareham Fotografie, Sally and Richard Greenhill, The National Trust Photolibrary, epa european pressphoto agency b.v., Karol Kozlowski Premium RM Collection, Imagestate Media Partners Limited - Impact Photos, Universal Images Group North America LLC / DeAgostini, Magdalena Mayo; COMSTOCK; COVER; GETTY IMAGES SALES SPAIN/Erik Isakson/Tetra Images, Thinkstock/Jochen Sand, Toronto Star Archives, istock/Thinkstock, Adrian Weinbrecht, Photos.com Plus, TothGaborGyula, Paulo Fridman, Morsa Images, Alison Buck, stefanamer, Thinkstock, Jacobs Stock Photography, Bloomberg, Auscape; HIGHRES PRESS STOCK/AbleStock.com; I. PREYSLER; ISTOCKPHOTO/digitalskillet, sunstock, YvanDube, ImageGap, DarthArt, Getty Images Sales Spain; REX SHUTTERSTOCK/Max Lakner/BFA, Eugene Adebari, Tnt/BFA.com, Snap Stills, Howard/ANL; SETH POPPEL YEARBOOK LIBRARY; SHUTTERSTOCK/Sky Designs, Dean Drobot, Fotocrisis; STOCKBYTE; Jim Benjaminson Collections via the Plymouth Bulletin; Samsung; SERIDEC PHOTOIMAGENES CD; J. Lucas; M. Sánchez; Prats i Camps; 123RF; ALAMY/Blend Images, INTERFOTO, REUTERS, Keith Homan, MBI, imageBROKER, Jose Luis Suerte, Harold Smith, Ian Allenden, Peter Horree, MS Bretherton, Pulsar Images, andy lane, Nano Calvo, Radharc Images, Westend61 GmbH, Colin Underhill, Gianni Muratore, Mary Evans Picture Library, Michael Wheatley, Alibi Productions, a-plus image bank, ONOKY - Photononstop, Directphoto Collection, Arterra Picture Library, Martin Thomas Photography, Agencja Fotograficzna Caro, Cathy Topping, Blend Images - BUILT Content, Geraint Lewis; GETTY IMAGES SALES SPAIN/Thinkstock; I. PREYSLER; ISTOCKPHOTO/Getty Images Sales Spain; SHUTTERSTOCK; SHUTTERSTOCK NETHERLANDS,B.V.; SOUTHWEST NEWS/Leicester Mercury; ARCHIVO SANTILLANA

Cover Photo: istockphoto/wundervisuals

We would like to thank the following reviewers for their valuable feedback which has made Personal Best possible. We extend our thanks to the many teachers and students not mentioned here.
Brad Bawtinheimer, Manuel Hidalgo, Paulo Dantas, Diana Bermúdez, Laura Gutiérrez, Hardy Griffin, Angi Conti, Christopher Morabito, Hande Kokce, Jorge Lobato, Leonardo Mercato, Mercilinda Ortiz, Wendy López

The Publisher has made every effort to trace the owner of copyright material; however, the Publisher will correct any involuntary omission at the earliest opportunity.

Printed in Mexico by Impregráfica Digital, S.A. de C.V. Calle España 385, Col. San Nicolás Tolentino, C.P. 09850, Iztapalapa, Ciudad de México. August, 2018